FORD Differentials

How to Rebuild the 8.8 and 9 Inch

Joseph Palazzolo

CarTech®

CarTech®

CarTech®, Inc.
6118 Main Street
North Branch, MN 55056
Phone: 651-277-1200 or 800-551-4754
Fax: 651-277-1203
www.cartechbooks.com

Edit by Paul Johnson
Layout by Monica Seiberlich

ISBN 978-1-61325-038-9
Item No. SA249

Library of Congress Cataloging-in-Publication Data

Palazzolo, Joseph.
   Ford differentials : how to rebuild the 8.8 and 9 inch / By Joseph Palazzolo.
     p. cm.
   ISBN 978-1-61325-038-9
1. Ford automobile--Differentials--Maintenance and repair--Handbooks, manuals, etc. 2. Ford automobile--Axles--Maintenance and repair--Handbooks, manuals, etc. I. Title.

   TL215.F7P35 2013
   629.2'45--dc23

                    2012045860

Written, edited, and designed in the U.S.A.
Printed in China
10 9 8 7

Title Page: *An assortment of Ford 9-inch axle stampings is welded together to create the housing. The cast-iron third member is installed through the front of the housing. It supports all of the gear and bearings, which allows for easier gear ratio swaps, if you have multiple third members.*

Back Cover Photos

Top Left: *You need to carefully identify and inspect the differential when you're in the market to buy one. This case looks like a nodular unit from the front, regarding rib structure, but does not have the "N" on it. When you look on the inside, you see the WAB-4025A. This is not a nodular unit.*

Top Right: *The 8.8-inch pinion requires some shimming to set the correct pinion depth on the ring gear. Some aftermarket gears are marked; Ford Motorsports gears and original-equipment gears are not marked. In this case, the pinion head markings identify it.*

Middle Left: *A dial indicator is set up to verify backlash and pattern. Remember to check backlash in at least four different positions; there should not be more than .004-inch variation. Every new gear set should come with a backlash recommendation in the instructions.*

Middle Right: *The side gears have been installed. Once in place, the washer is set in position and assembly grease is applied to the face of the washer. When all of the differential internal pieces are in place the differential case halves can be closed.*

Bottom Left: *The ring gear is pulled into position and a couple of bolts are installed. Note the bolts have washers under the heads. These smaller headed bolts with washers are used in Traction-Lok applications only. Open differentials and most other aftermarket differentials use larger headed open differential style ring gear bolts.*

Bottom Right: *This Ford 9-inch differential assembly is nearly complete. The adjuster nuts need to be set in place. Extra care must be taken to be sure the threads are lined up correctly.*

DISTRIBUTION BY:

Europe
PGUK
63 Hatton Garden
London EC1N 8LE, England
Phone: 020 7061 1980 • Fax: 020 7242 3725
www.pguk.co.uk

Australia
Renniks Publications Ltd.
3/37-39 Green Street
Banksmeadow, NSW 2109, Australia
Phone: 2 9695 7055 • Fax: 2 9695 7355
www.renniks.com

Canada
Login Canada
300 Saulteaux Crescent
Winnipeg, MB, R3J 3T2 Canada
Phone: 800 665 1148 • Fax: 800 665 0103
www.lb.ca

CONTENTS

ACKNOWLEDGMENTS

This project has been a very challenging journey for me. Even though the 1957 Chevy highlighted in Chapter 8 is not my first car restoration, it proved to be frustrating at times to be writing while building a car. I sincerely thank everyone who helped either directly or indirectly with the writing of this book. With this text completed, hopefully now I can get the car completed.

First and foremost, I must thank my wife, Kathy, for persevering through yet another book project while juggling the demands of the household and our twin boys. It has proven to be quite a challenge for both of us. I am truly blessed to have such a kind woman in my life supporting this endeavor and me. You never reminded me how difficult this was on all of us and instead you offered support and continuous encouragement, even when I questioned why I was doing this again. This book has become a family affair that is not just my book but rather our book. Thank you.

The entire team at Currie Enterprises, specifically Brian Shephard, treated me like part of the extended family and opened up the entire shop, parts, and mechanics for this project. Without their knowledge and willingness to share, this book would have never been possible. There was never a time when they did not accommodate any of my many requests for support and help. The Currie team recognized the need for a Ford axle book and even helped push this book to hopefully be considered the ultimate reference.

I thank Earle Williams for all of the great support, producing truly awesome hardware, and even the shop tour and guidance on the car. It is people like Earle that make the performance and aftermarket industry great.

My good friend Tony Nausieda reviewed the text countless times for accuracy while working on his advanced degree. I am fortunate to have a friend who is willing to sacrifice sleep and his own projects to help out with this text.

My high school friend, John Hosta, for influencing my life and jointly learning how to build performance race cars. We had many trials and errors on our cars, but we learned together to never give up and always strive to build what we are capable of.

Mac Kirkwood for the countless hours of conversation and advice on different methods to present the information and reviewing the manuscript.

My good friends Nate Tovey and Gordon McIndoe for providing a ton of feedback and providing a last-minute photo studio and even shop space for storage.

Ray Kuczera for his support and willingness to help. He was always there to remind me through example how important it is to share as much information as possible with as many people as possible.

Of course, the teams at Currie, Williams Classic Chassis Works, Hellwig, McLeod, D&D Performance, Performance Online, and Tremec for their support, advice, and great products. Without aftermarket companies such as these, the car build would have never been possible.

I hope that I did not leave anyone out; I sincerely want to thank you all.

My twin sons, Christian (left) and Adrian (right) were great helpers throughout this project.

This book covers two of the most common Ford axles (8.8- and 9-inch) and the exact details on how to disassemble, inspect, upgrade, and build these axles into high-performing and reliable units. However, many of the principles can be applied to most other axles. I have performed hours of rebuilds and modifications of these units along with research and interviews with the experts to understand what works and what does not. Many magazines tend to skip over the modifications required to make an aftermarket part fit correctly. After reading this book, you should be better prepared to complete your Ford axle project.

My first experience repairing axles was with the front axle on a 1981 Buick Riviera. Like many of the parts of the car that I had previously worked on, it came out of necessity and curiosity. The necessity was more financial, as I could not afford to have a mechanic repair my cars and the curiosity was that I really wanted to understand how these things work.

The Riviera has a north/south powertrain layout with an Oldsmobile 350 V-8, a unique transmission, and an independent-style front axle next to the engine's oil pan. Numerous Mustang 7.5- and 8.8-inch rear axles and then GM 10- and 12-bolt axles quickly followed it. There have been countless repairs of vehicles since then including quick-change-style axles and all of the Dana variants, including Corvettes and Vipers.

Have a conversation with any muscle car or street rod enthusiast, and when it comes to axles, most will swear by the Ford 9-inch axle. It has been the *go to* axle for decades. Even with production stopped more than 25 years ago, this axle still has a place in many performance cars and trucks. It seems that rear axles are a bit of a mystery even to the most veteran of mechanics. While we are comfortable with engines, brakes, and suspension, few are comfortable working on and setting up axles at home. I am not certain if this is because most axles only require minor maintenance to be trouble-free, and therefore, mechanics don't get enough practice to stay sharp or if it is from a bad experience of working on an axle. The latter is probably why most shops do not want to work on them and leave them to the specialists or experts.

My intention is to help you understand the function of and how to rebuild the Ford 8.8- and 9-inch axles. With this knowledge, you can decide whether you want to tackle your axle repair yourself or at least understand what is involved and how to find a good shop to perform the work for you.

Axles are the only part of a car that utilize a hypoid gear set. These gears require some special training, tools, and skill to work on correctly. That being said, it is not beyond most competent mechanics and even the enthusiast to repair or rebuild axles. As with any car repair, this requires

organization, time, and patience. But with these in place, most mechanics can achieve great results.

When it comes to gear ratio, this book should help you decide if 4.10s make sense based on your vehicle's transmission ratios, tire size, and intended usage. It will also help you decide if you really need 35-tooth spline axle shafts.

You need be sure that the upgrades you make meet your end objectives and don't just waste your hard-earned time and money. I have received countless calls and emails from people who purchased the wrong hardware, have it in their car and are unhappy because someone gave them bad advice. It is so important to understand your project and select the correct components to have your desired outcome.

I provide information that you won't find in a common shop manual while still covering the shop manual fundamentals. I want to be as comprehensive as possible but I cannot include every single piece of information on these Ford axles. I have, however, tried to make certain that all of the facts in this book are correct.

So when someone provides you with *good advice* like *"a Ford 9-inch with 4.11s is the best way to go for your car,"* take it with a grain of salt and do your own research to get the best solution for your needs. The key is to enjoy the work and with the help of this book, you will achieve great results.

WHAT IS A WORKBENCH® BOOK?

This Workbench® Series book is the only book of its kind on the market. No other book offers the same combination of detailed hands-on information and revealing color photographs to illustrate differential rebuilding. Rest assured, you have purchased an indispensable companion that will expertly guide you, one step at a time, through each important stage of the rebuilding process. This book is packed with real-world techniques and practical tips for expertly performing rebuild procedures, not vague instructions or unnecessary processes. At-home mechanics or enthusiast builders strive for professional results, and the instruction in our Workbench® Series books help you realize pro-caliber results. Hundreds of photos guide you through the entire process from start to finish, with informative captions containing comprehensive instructions for every step of the process.

The step-by-step photo procedures also contain many additional photos that show how to install high-performance components, modify stock components for special applications, or even call attention to assembly steps that are critical to proper operation or safety. These are labeled with unique icons. These symbols represent an idea, and photos marked with the icons contain important, specialized information.

Here are some of the icons found in Workbench® books:

***Important!*–** Calls special attention to a step or procedure, so that the procedure is correctly performed. This prevents damage to a vehicle, system, or component.

***Save Money*–** Illustrates a method or alternate method of performing a rebuild step that will save money but still give acceptable results.

***Torque Fasteners*–** Illustrates a fastener that must be properly tightened with a torque wrench at this point in the rebuild. The torque specs are usually provided in the step.

***Special Tool*–** Illustrates the use of a special tool that may be required or can make the job easier (caption with photo explains further).

***Performance Tip*–** Indicates a procedure or modification that can improve performance. Step most often applies to high-performance or racing engines.

***Critical Inspection*–** Indicates that a component must be inspected to ensure proper operation of the engine.

***Precision Measurement*–** Illustrates a precision measurement or adjustment that is required at this point in the rebuild.

***Professional Mechanic Tip*–** Illustrates a step in the rebuild that non-professionals may not know. It may illustrate a shortcut, or a trick to improve reliability, prevent component damage, etc.

***Documentation Required*–** Illustrates a point in the rebuild where the reader should write down a particular measurement, size, part number, etc. for later reference or photograph a part, area or system of the vehicle for future reference.

***Tech Tip*–** Tech Tips provide brief coverage of important subject matter that doesn't naturally fall into the text or step-by-step procedures of a chapter. Tech Tips contain valuable hints, important info, or outstanding products that professionals have discovered after years of work. These will add to your understanding of the process, and help you get the most power, economy, and reliability from your engine.

AXLE HISTORY AND IDENTIFICATION

Before you embark on the rebuild and start scouring local scrap yards and online websites, it will be helpful to understand what to look for and what to avoid in these axles.

First, you need to understand some fundamentals of the Ford axles to help guide your quest. I have spent countless hours over the years collecting, reading, and studying old shop manuals, supplier reference documents, SAE papers, and even vehicle manufacturer reports and notes. Some of this information is very important as it is becoming more and more difficult to find documentation on axles and differentials that were built more than 40 years ago. I have also spent many hours in scrap yards and visiting and interviewing the experts in this field along with years of building numerous axles myself. In this chapter I share a summary of decades of work on these axles.

As part of my research, I went to renowned Currie Enterprises and gathered one of just about every different 9-inch axle variant. I put together a whole collection of housings and third members. This is a sampling of some of them. Here is a quick visual summary: The 1957 housings do not have dimples on them and have an oil drain plug. The 1958s and 1959s have two dimples on either side of the housing and some have drain plugs. The 1960s to 1967s still retain the dimples but also have an oil level plug in the back cover.

The Ford 8.8-inch axle has a cast center section and the internal components are installed from the rear. There is typically a stamped steel cover that must be removed to gain access to the internals.

Flange-to-Flange Width *(inches)*	Application	Flange-to-Flange Width *(inches)*	Application
56.375	1974–1977 Maverick (8- and 9-inch axle) 1970-up Comet 1964–1965 Falcon	58.000	1966–1977 Bronco 1977–1981 Granada/ Versailles
56.875	1974–1977 Mustang II (8-inch axle)	59.375	1967–1970 Mustang 1967–1970 Cougar 1967–1970 Fairlane
57.250	1957–1959 Ranchero 1957–1959 Station Wagon	60.875	1971–1973 Mustang
		63.375	1967–1973 Torino
		68.000	1972 3/4-ton Van
57.375	1964½–1966 Mustang 1967–1969 Comet		

This chart serves as a general guideline for axle flange-to-flange width based on different models and production years. I have included the narrow 8-inch axles for reference. The narrowest production 9-inch axle is 56.375 inches. If measuring the drum-to-drum distance, add .200-inch to these values.

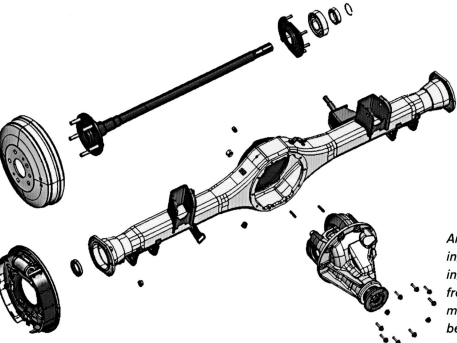

There is a very fundamental difference between Ford's 8.8- and 9-inch axles. I reference these axles based on the ring gear nominal outside diameter in inches. The fundamental difference between these axles is how the gears are supported and which end of the axle housing (front or back) that they are assembled from.

8-Inch

It may seem strange to begin by comparing the 8-inch to the 9-inch axle, but there is an important distinction to make since the 8-inch axle is weaker than the 9-inch. Many people are not aware that Ford made a smaller banjo axle and confuse the 8-inch for a 9-inch.

The 8-inch was introduced in 1962 and is found in many lower performance Fairlanes, Mustangs, Falcons, Comets, Cougars, and Pintos, just to name a few of the applications.

There's an easy way to tell an 8-inch apart from a 9-inch. All of the 8-inch case nuts can be accessed with a socket. In contrast, on the 9-inch, two nuts on the bottom at about the 6 and 7 o'clock positions cannot be accessed with a socket and require a wrench.

Both axles share a common design and are often referred to as banjo style or third-member style. The smaller 8-inch just cannot handle the abuse as its bigger brother can. The 8-inch also was only available with 28-tooth axle shafts. Unless you are building a

An assortment of Ford 9-inch axle stampings is welded together to create the housing. The cast-iron third member is installed from the front of the housing. The third member supports all of the gears and bearings, which allows for easier gear ratio swaps if you have multiple third members.

The smaller 8-inch third member is on the right. Note the two lower bolts at 6 and 7 o'clock have straight access with a socket. The 9-inch third-member bottom fasteners, on the left, can only be accessed with a wrench. This is an easy way to identify the third members, so you're sure to buy the correct axle.

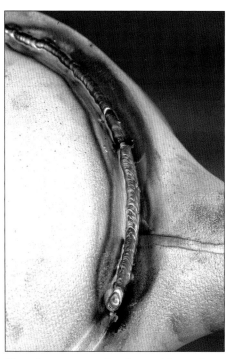

Here is an example of a weld repair on a factory original housing. It was required to repair a leaking weld. The repair process requires the axle to be disassembled and thoroughly cleaned. The leaking weld area is then ground down and a MIG or TIG welder is used for the repair. This is a relatively common issue on these housings.

Pinto or straight six-cylinder vehicle, you want to avoid it.

Both 8- and 9-inch axle housings are made from a series of stampings that are fixtured and welded together. This complex fixturing and welding process, coupled with fuel economy concerns, is what eventually led to their production demise. These axles had a stout 2.25-inch ring gear offset as compared to a 1.5-inch ring gear offset of the later 8.8-inch axle.

The larger offset is better for strength and noise but worse for sliding and efficiency. While the larger offset makes the ring and pinion gears stronger, the additional sliding of the gear teeth creates more heat in the axle. Therefore, these axle assemblies require better quality oil and good underbody airflow to keep the unit cool. With their high-volume production, the two biggest quality problems were leaks from poor welds and poor alignment of the housings. So don't be surprised that most of these axles leak from the welds. Careful aftermarket shops and their stringent attention to repairing these housings are able to correct many of these issues.

9-Inch

The Ford 9-inch has a reputation as a durable axle that can transmit enormous torque, and this is rightfully deserved. Some even consider these axles to be bulletproof. This is by far the most common axle used by restorers, hot rodders, customizers, and racers. It has enjoyed a long production history with many variants. There is a huge aftermarket support for this axle design. Many companies, such as Currie Enterprises, Mark Williams Enterprises, Moser Engineering, and Strange Engineering, reproduce this design today. It is still used in NASCAR racing as well.

Because of the long production history of this axle, many variants are available. Most of the time, the differences are in shock and spring

The straddle-mounted pinion has a roller bearing in the gear case, which provides additional support for the pinion under heavy loads. This bearing and the casting structure surrounding it need to be carefully inspected as this is a common area for cracks.

This pinion has the tapered bearings and collapsible spacer in place. The bearing cups are in the pinion cartridge and the third bearing trunnion roller bearing is located in the gear case. This pinion shows excessive wear on the trunnion surface and should not be re-used.

mounting brackets and, of course, brake hardware. It is a banjo-style axle as is the 8-inch. It was in production on many Ford cars and trucks, first appearing in 1957 and finally replaced by the Salisbury-style 8.8-inch axle in 1986, saving about 50 pounds and boasting increased efficiency.

Pinion Offset

The 9-inch's very large pinion offset of 2.25 inches requires the pinion to be straddle mounted, which refers to the fact the pinion head has bearings that straddle it on either side. There is a machined roller bearing race on the pinion head portion that points at the differential opposite the tapered bearing races. This additional bearing and, more importantly, the necessary casting support structure is what drives the larger hypoid offset. The additional straddle mount pocket bearing provides additional support to the pinion head during high-torque events. This bearing is one of the reasons that the 9-inch has the reputation for being bulletproof.

There are three bearings on the pinion shaft: the two traditional tapered roller bearings for the head and tail bearings with a third cylindrical roller bearing on the opposite end of the pinion head. In order to allow for the additional straddle mounted bearing and casting support structure, the hypoid offset

needs to be large enough to clear the differential case. Hypoid offset is the distance between the centerline of the pinion and the centerline of the ring gear. This is 2.25 inches for the Ford 9-inch and 1.5 inches for the 8.8-inch axle.

Identification Tag

People have been climbing around scrap yards for years to find the best examples of the 9-inch axle. If you are fortunate enough to find an axle with the identification tag still attached, it will help solve part of the mystery of what application the axle came from and what might still be inside.

The axle identification tag is located at about the 3 o'clock position under the third-member mounting nut when you are looking straight at the front of the axle. These tags are typically quite beat up, twisted, and rusted over the years. These tags were not that infor-

This is a typical axle tag that has been removed from the third member. The code, 4L11, tells us that it is a 4.11:1 ratio with a limited-slip or Traction-Lok differential. It also has a 9-inch ring gear.

mative on the early units, so from 1957 to 1962 the tag just referenced axle ratio. In 1963, Ford included more information.

The axle tag typically has two lines of numbers and letters stamped on it. The format has changed over the years but mostly follow this sequence:. The top line typically starts with a three-digit axle model code (or the prefix of the part number), followed by a dash, and then the suffix. The axle model codes are interchangeable, typically the suffixes are different for a revision change but the axle is still interchangeable with one having the previous suffix. There may be a second dash and more numbers and letters on the top row if there are specifics that are unique for interchange information. Typically with just this information, you can cross reference what you need to know about the axle. The last set of digits on the top row on the right side is the date code.

The bottom line begins with the ratio being the first set of numbers. If an L is included, it was equipped with a limited-slip differential or Traction-Lok. The middle number is the ring gear diameter in inches, typically an 8 or 9. The last set of numbers is the vehicle plant code.

If the axle tag is missing, as most are, you need to remove the third member in order to know what ratio you have and if it has a limited-slip or not.

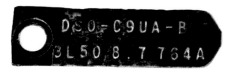

This custom axle tag was obviously hand cut as evidenced by the sharp tin-snipped-looking ends and includes DSO, for Dealer Special Order. Notice that the date code is C9UA with the ring gear size of 8.7. This was an 8.75-inch ring gear in a 9-inch housing. These were used sporadically until about 1969. You can install a true 9-inch gear in these housings as well.

Don't be surprised if the tag you have does not exactly match this. There are also unique domestic special-option tags, which don't follow the format.

Date Code

The date code is stamped on the tag. The first number is the last digit of the model year of the decade, the next digit is a letter and represents the month (A is for January, B is for February, and so on), and the last two digits represent the day of the month. This format is also applicable to casting date codes.

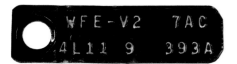

The date code on this axle tag is 7AC, and it corresponds to the 7th year, 1st month (January), and 3rd day. The WFE-V2 helps us find the decade of the 1970s. This axle tag belongs to a 1977 F-150.

This chart references the connection between the month codes and the actual month. The letters I and O are skipped to avoid confusion with the numbers one and zero.

Some tags reference the week of the month instead of the exact day and just use a letter (A to E) for first through the fifth week of the month.

Case Type

You are looking for a nodular iron case, with its telltale "N" cast into the front or inside wall. These third members are the strongest of the production cases and the most desired. Aftermarket vendors are actually re-casting these cases in very strong nodular iron, so more often than not it is easiest just to purchase a new case.

But if you're looking for an original, they can be spotted quite readily even without an axle identification tag. The N cases had two vertical ribs, three horizontal ribs, and a machined-in fill plug. There are four versions of the nodular iron third members that were produced from the factory. These first became available on the 1964 Galaxies with

A metal axle tag is typically located on the driver-side front of the third member. It is underneath one of the nuts that holds the third member in place. In most cases, the tag has been lost. On this particular third member, the original copper washers that were under the factory fasteners have been discarded as well.

the 427-ci engine and were found on many higher horsepower cars and trucks.

Of the four versions of the N case, three have an actual "N" cast into it right above the pinion cartridge.

The fourth version did not have the "N" in the casting on the outside but still retained the rib structure. In order to verify a nodular unit, you need to look on the inside of the casting. These have a C4AW-4025-B casting part number next to the adjuster nut.

Of course, if your budget allows, you can purchase an aftermarket iron case that is stronger than any factory case. If you are looking for an N case or think that you have found one of these desirable axles, make certain to examine it closely. The WAR, WAA, and WAB cases have the same ribbing as the N case, but are missing the ever important "N" feature.

Any of the W-series cases do have a fill plug machined in them. Both standard and W-series cases are made out of gray cast iron. Only the

Month Code ID											
First year month codes											
A	B	C	D	E	F	G	H	J	K	L	M
Jan	Feb	Mar	Apr	May	Jun	Jul	Aug	Sep	Oct	Nov	Dec
Second year month codes											
N	P	Q	R	S	T	U	V	W	X	Y	Z
Jan	Feb	Mar	Apr	May	Jun	Jul	Aug	Sep	Oct	Nov	Dec

N-series cases are made out of the stronger, more desirable, nodular iron. While the iron is molten, magnesium is added to increase the shear strength of the alloy. The magnesium addition causes the grain structure to change from flakes to nodules and thus the name "nodular" iron. The N cases typically came with the larger Daytona-style pinion support bearing, and 31-spline axle shafts.

Pinion Cartridge

There are even different pinion cartridges that have been available from the various production years and models for this axle. The Daytona-style cartridge allows for a larger pinion head bearing when compared to the standard pinion cartridge. This is a great upgrade component to use for high-power applications or if you are replacing your cartridge.

Housing

Like most Ford axles, the 9-inch has a single hypoid ring gear mounting distance, so, unlike the Dana and GM axles that require unique differ-

This case looked like a nodular unit from the front regarding rib structure but did not have the "N" on it. When you look on the inside, you see WAB-4025A. This is not a nodular unit.

The desirable N-style, nodular-iron gear cases are available in four different versions. There are three versions with external Ns cast in; note the more curved style on the top right. The unit on the top left seems to be nodular iron but requires a little more investigation to verify.

ential carriers based on ratio, a single differential carrier works with all of the Ford ratios. Also, since this axle is used in so many circle-track race cars, the 9-inch enjoys an unparalleled availability of different gear ratios in the aftermarket.

This is when making a few phone calls to reputable axle build-

The aftermarket Daytona-style pinion cartridge accommodates the larger and stronger pinion head bearing. This particular pinion cartridge is well reinforced and much stronger than the stock production cartridge.

Here are the internal sides of the same three units. Now you can see the C4AW-4025-B part number on the lower left unit, which verifies it as a nodular unit.

ers can be helpful. There are quite a few companies making Ford 9-inch housings to fit just about any muscle car out there, including non-Ford vehicles. (See Chapter 8 for how to install a 9-inch in a classic 1957 Chevy Bel Air as a performance upgrade.)

The axle housings themselves had many different variations over time as well. These variations include different-size drum brakes, disc brakes, and wheel hub arrangements.

Since these housings were a series of stamped-steel pieces all welded together, there were many different overall lengths, tubes sections, mounting brackets, and even general constructions over the years (see Chapter 5).

8.8-Inch

The Ford 8.8-inch is very similar to the General Motors (GM) 8⅞-inch, 12-bolt axle. Some differential experts tell you that the Blue Oval engineers copied the 12-bolt design when they came up with the

8.8-inch axle. While the 8.8 is similar to the 12-bolt, it isn't identical. Interestingly, the Ford axle uses the exact same size of tapered roller bearings as the GM 12-bolt. The Ford version uses larger axle shafts and different lube flow strategy. These axles did have metal axle tags similar to the 9-inch axles but they were slowly phased out as vehicle programs were updated. There are several reasons for this.

Cost and complexity are two. These tags provided information for the service technicians but wasn't that important for the vehicle assembly plants. The third reason was basic health and safety concerns for the assembly technicians and other employees who handled the axles in the manufacturing and assembly plants. There were many instances of

cuts and scratches from the thin steel tags sticking up on the axles.

The tags were replaced with adhesive labels that are placed around the

This is an example of the brakes that fit the small wheel end bearing for a 10 x 2-inch-wide drum brake on the left and a 10 x 1¾-inch on the right.

Axle Flange Sizes

Symbol	Description	Large Bearing Flange (inches)	Small Bearing Flange (inches)	Torino Style Bearing Flange (inches)
A	Horizontal Bolt Spacing	3.500	3.3125	3.5625
B	Vertical Bolt Spacing	2.375	2.0000	2.00
C	Inside Diameter	3.150	2.8350	3.150
D	Bolt Clearance Hole	1/2, 7/16, 3/8	3/8	3/8

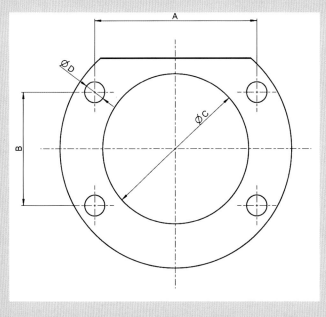

The chart above summarizes the three flange-style dimensions for currently available units. The large bearing flange can have any of the three sizes of clearance holes listed. The 3/8-inch holes were found on the 1978–1979 model year pick-up trucks, Broncos, and some Lincoln Versailles; the 1/2-inch clearance hole is the most common; and the 7/16-inch hole is extremely rare.

The diagram at left shows the typical wheel-end flange configuration. There are various different outside shapes. Some have a D-shape, full circles, and two flats, and while others have five holes instead of four.

Here is an example of 11 x 2¼-inch drums brakes with the small bearing size on the left and the large Torino style on the right.

axle tube near the brake and wheel end. These labels have a specific code that is similar to the axle code on the 9-inch axles.

The Ford 8.8-inch axle has the same ring gear mounting distance (see Chapter 7) for all ratios, just like the 9-inch. So again, unlike the GM and Dana axles that require a unique differential with different ratios, the Ford 8.8-inch differential is common across all of the ring-and-pinion ratios. There is a ton of aftermarket support for this axle (see Chapters 3 and 4 for more details).

The 8.8 is a traditional semi-float Salisbury axle with C-washers for axle retention. Many people prefer to just call it the Ford 9-inch-style wheel end. But to be correct, it is a 3/4 float. There are 8.5-inch gears installed in these housings for lower-power vehicle applications. The

The large bearing size was available with five different brake drum widths. Four of the 11-inch-diameter versions are pictured: 1¾ inches (top left), 2¼ inches (top right), 2½ inches (bottom left), and 3 inches (bottom right). A 2-inch version is not shown.

Along with the many different brake and wheel end varieties, many different styles of axle shaft ends were manufactured. Some have only one access hole for the backing plate bolts, while others have three. Most have the two driving holes for the manufacturing process while one has a more square looking drive end. None of which changes the strength of the axle shaft. There are even different drum brake registers.

The Lincoln Continental style of disc brakes use 11½-inch rotors. In the 1980s and 1990s, the Lincoln Versailles brakes and complete axles were highly sought after because it was the only way to get a 9-inch axle with discs in a 58-inch-wide axle package. At this width, many were used in street rod applications without modification. With so many better performing after-market options today, there is no reason to use these marginal brakes.

Some axle shafts can be shortened and a new spline machined in place. The 28-tooth axle shafts are typically tapered and cannot be shortened. Most 1972 and earlier 31-tooth spline shafts can be shortened and 1973 and later versions typically cannot be resplined. Here is a picture of the milling machine cutting new spline teeth after the axle has been cut to length.

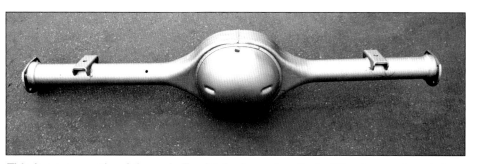

This is an example of the only Ford 9-inch version that utilized one-piece tubes. Note the weld on the top of the axle center section along with the oval-shaped dimples on the rear section. The tubes do not have any welds, and you just see the witness marks of the parting line for the dies on the tubes. This was offered on the 1960 F-100 truck.

The Mustang Shelby GT housing is an easy one to spot, albeit rare, because it has extreme tapering of the axle tubes at the ends. There was a desire to have the stronger, larger tubes near the center of the axle but still retain the narrower tube ends for the wheel ends and the unique Shelby suspension brackets.

Besides the styling of the Ford Edsel, even the axle shafts were very unusual. These shafts had a longer brake spacing offset and a unique brake drum register diameter of 2.870 inches, which was uncommon for the time. (It was later used for pick-ups and Broncos.) These axles even have a unique bolt pattern of five on 5 inches. I guess this helps add to the splendor of the vehicle.

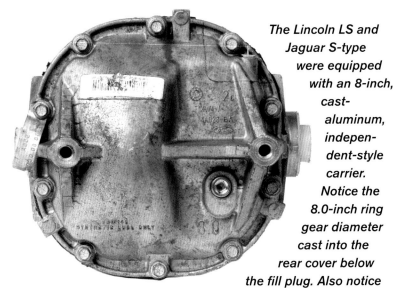

From my piles of rare parts, here is an independent cast-iron 8.8-inch carrier axle. Note the ring diameter cast into the housing above the pinion.

The Lincoln LS and Jaguar S-type were equipped with an 8-inch, cast-aluminum, independent-style carrier. Notice the 8.0-inch ring gear diameter cast into the rear cover below the fill plug. Also notice the part number and metal axle tag. The bar code is present on this unit as well, although later axles just carry the bar code and the metal tag is no longer required.

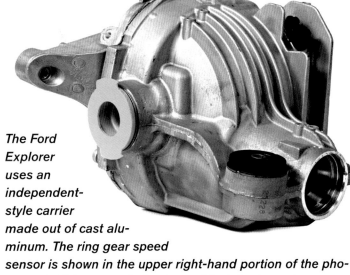

Ironically, 8.0-inch independent carriers were made in cast iron. Here is an example of such a unit.

The Ford Explorer uses an independent-style carrier made out of cast aluminum. The ring gear speed sensor is shown in the upper right-hand portion of the photograph. This sensor is for the anti-lock brake system.

typical 3-inch-diameter tubes can be a bit flimsy in higher-power applications.

The 8.5- and 8.8-inch gears have even found themselves in the independent-carrier-style axles. The Ford Mustang and Thunderbird used this style for a few model years. There were also 8-inch ring gear independent carriers in production.

Front Axle Applications

While the majority of this book focuses on rear-wheel-drive applications, there are also four-wheel-drive applications of the Ford 8.8-inch and 9-inch axles. When used in these applications the axles are very similar to a rear axle except they have a different wheel end arrangement that allows for the steering knuckles to be mounted.

When these axles are used to drive the front wheels, the hypoid gear set is basically flipped over and special reverse-cut tooth geometry is utilized for the 8.8-inch version. Reverse cut just means that the spiral hand is the opposite of traditional ring gears for a rear axle application; it is the mirror image of a standard rear axle gear (see Chapter 3).

This means that the standard 8.8-inch rear axle gears cannot be used for a front axle application and vice versa. During the manufacturing process, the gear blank forgings and the gear design are the same; just the spiral angle is machined to the opposite hand.

Reverse-Rotation Gear Set

The most common 8.8-inch front axle application is the F-150/Expedition platform. Four-wheel-drive vehicles use a unique reverse-rotation-style hypoid gear set, and the pinion is set above center on the front axle. With the pinion in that location, a special provision is required to supply adequate lubrication to the pinion bearings.

The production axle is an independent-style axle arrangement with halfshafts to the drive the wheels. The stub shafts that come out of the aluminum axle housing are a 28-tooth spline shaft. These 28-tooth side gears in the differential are unique as they have a snap-ring groove machined

in them to retain the stub shafts and do not rely on C-washer retention as does the rear axle version. The main reason for the pinion to be above center is to reduce the angles on the front propshaft universal joints.

This special 8.8-inch, reverse-cut-style gear set is also used on the Currie high-pinion, 9-inch axles. They have unique cast gear cases that accommodate the smaller 8.8-inch offset but still retain the 9-inch-style differential and bearing support structure for the ring gear. The pinion is not the traditional cartridge style as on the common 9-inch; it actually operates similar to the 8.8-inch-style gear set.

Straddle-Mount Pinion Bearing

Another difference between the 8.8-inch arrangement and the traditional 9-inch is that the 8.8-inch gears do not have the trunnion on the pinion head, so the high-pinion 9-inch axles do not have the straddle-mounted pinion bearing arrangement. Therefore, the high-pinion, 9-inch axle used for off-road and

lifted truck applications is more of a hybrid combination of the 9-inch structure with 8.8-inch gears. This axle assembly usually drives 35-inch tires and transmits up to 400 hp. The hybrid third member can also be used in the rear axle application, again limiting power and tire size. The high-pinion third members have some unique features added to the gear case in order to catch and direct oil to the bearings.

It is possible to use a traditional 9-inch rear axle third member and just flip it over to drive the front wheels. But in this configuration, the hypoid gears are typically driving on the coast side of the gears, which are not as strong, with a typical reduction in load-carrying capacity of about 20 to 30 percent along with poor oil flow.

9-inch Gear Arrangement

Hi9 has developed an actual 9-inch gear arrangement, also called TrueHi9. Again, the pinion located above center helps with driveshaft angles and ground clearance, but it requires unique oil porting and baffling in order to catch and feed oil to the pinion bearings. This arrangement uses a unique 9-inch-style gear set, produced by Richmond Gear, that has the reverse-cut method to drive on the drive side of the gear tooth faces.

Hi9 also offers the MegaHi9. It uses gears that are made out of the stronger SAE9310 material (as compared to SAE 8620), along with a 35-tooth splined pinion arrangement. The material change makes the gears approximately 15 percent stronger.

The TrueHi9 design has a distinctive thrust button feature to help combat ring gear separating forces

From left to right are: 10-inch, 9-inch, and GM G-Body 7.5-inch 10-bolt.

Here is a comparison of pinions from a 10-inch ring and pinion set with a 35-tooth spline (left) and a stock 9-inch pinion with a 28-tooth spline (right).

along with a unique reinforced gear case in the pinion pocket bearing area. This thrust button is just a hardened, threaded, adjustable support that is very close to the ring gear back face. When the ring gear deflects from high-torque loads, the thrust button surface actually contacts a specially machined surface on the back face of the ring gear and resists that deflection.

Both the TrueHi9 and the MegaHi9 units use the 9-inch-style differential, which means that all aftermarket differential options can be used in these axle housings. These axles are common upgrades for Jeep Wranglers and Ford Broncos.

10-inch Gear Arrangement

Recently, a unique 10-inch diameter gear set has been developed (for the off-road Trophy Truck market) that fits in the 9-inch-style gear case. It provides even more strength and torque-carrying capacity of the gears. Unique yokes are required for this arrangement because it has a larger 35-tooth spline as compared to the 28-tooth standard 9-inch pinion yoke. The axle housing requires some minor machining to obtain clearance for the larger ring gear.

These gears are massive and special for racing applications, so the ratios are limited; even the gears are expensive. A typical cost for one of these hypoid gear sets can easily be in the $1,100 range and ratio availability is sporadic. If a specific ratio demand slows down, then the ratio

is no longer produced until demand picks back up. Once the demand reaches a certain level, a run of a specific ratio is made. Typically the following have been or are available: 4.11, 4.29, 4.71, 5.00, 5.14, 5.29, 5.37, and 5.43:1. Due to the high cost associated with producing these gears availability is ever changing.

Off-Road Upgrade

A unique 7075 billet-aluminum pinion cartridge with a washer and retainer ring, which are installed after the pinion seal, is another common upgrade for off-road applications. This setup is typically used with the 10-inch gear. The positive retention helps to protect the seal and makes certain that the pinion seal does not pop out of the cartridge during off-road use. This setup is often used on units installed in Trophy race trucks.

A previous version of this style of seal retention just used bolts to retain the pinion seal. That style was a little better than just the seal alone but was not ideal. The seal was still vulnerable to damage from

This is a typical modified pinion cartridge. It has bolts with washers to hold the seal in place.

This is a much better improvement over the bolted-style retention. It uses a counter-sunk retaining ring arrangement to better retain the seal in place.

The 9⅜-inch third member is often mistaken as a 9-inch. The top horizontal rib curving down on the right side is the easy indicator of this imposter. This axle has no aftermarket support for parts or upgrades and is not a good candidate for any performance application. The only reason to utilize this axle would be if you are performing an all-original restoration.

hitting something from the top or bottom. Typically the seal then pivots on the bolts and still ends up failing. The counter-sunk retaining ring arrangement from Currie Enterprises cured all of these potential failure situations.

9⅜-Inch

The Ford 9⅜-inch axle is often mistaken as a 9-inch. A 9⅜-inch axle has an obvious visual difference in the third-member casting rib structure of the curved top horizontal rib. Carefully inspect the axle, so you do not buy the wrong one. There's more than a few of these at swap meets and scrap yards that may be unknowingly misrepresented as a 9-inch, and these axles are not ideal for high-performance applications. Therefore, don't make the mistake and assume that every Ford banjo-style axle is a 9-inch. The age-old

advice applies—buyer beware—as these axles have very few parts interchangeable with the 9-inch.

The 9⅜-inch axle can typically be found on 1961 to about 1972 larger cars, such as the Lincolns and LTDs, and the high-powered pickup trucks from about the mid 1960s to the mid 1970s. These axles had large carrier bearings with an outside diameter of 3.265 inches. Some of these use the unique 3.250-inch outside-diameter wheel end bearings as compared to the typical large bearings, which are 3.150 inches. These axles are still not as strong as nodular iron 9-inch axles. There is no aftermarket support for these axles, so there's no reason to buy one for a high-performance or racing application. Therefore, the only reason to use one of these is for a concours-type restoration for originality.

There are no performance upgrades so you are stuck with used

parts or, if you are lucky, new old stock. As a result, I highly recommend that you avoid this axle for any performance application build-ups. You will be better off in the long run.

But there is one good side to this axle; you can swap the third member with a 9-inch unit and retain the rest. So if your vehicle already has this housing and you want to upgrade the gears and differential, you have choices. You can even put the larger 9⅜-inch third member in a 9-inch housing but you need to machine some additional ring gear clearance in the axle housing. The bolt pattern for the third member is common between the two axle housings. I am not sure why you would ever want to do that but it is physically possible.

Part Numbers

I could not review the history and identification of these axles without talking about the Ford part numbering system. The Ford part numbering system is well organized and structured as compared to some other original equipment manufacturers' systems that just utilize the "next number in sequence" philosophy.

Ford part numbers typically have three components: the prefix (three or four alpha-numeric characters) then a dash, followed by the basic number, another dash, and then the suffix or revision version. In some situations, there is even a pre-prefix with a single or double digit to help provide further clarification of the part's history.

Let's look at the part number for the nodular third member that I referenced earlier as an example:

C4AW-4025-B

The first character is for the decade and the second digit is the year of that specific decade. The second digit is also for the year of introduction or year of last revision.

All of the above holds true until the year 1999. It appears with the Y2K scare and other factors, Ford decided to revamp its date code strategy. Parts released in 1999 and forward follow this format:

The second and third characters are for the vehicle model code. For example, R3 is Mustang, H7 is F-Series Short Cab, L3 is F150/250.

Ford Part Number
First Character
(8.8- & 9-Inch Axle ID)

First Character	Decade
A	1940 (often omitted)
B	1950
C	1960
D	1970
E	1980
F	1990

Ford Part Number
Second Character
(8.8- & 9-Inch Axle ID)

Second Year Digit	Second Year Digit
0	6
1	7
2	8
3	9
4	
5	

This is a year-of-manufacture table for differentials. The first character is the decade, from 1940 to 1990, while the second is the year in that decade. So our example (C4AW-4025-B) was introduced in 1964.

Ford Part Number
Third Character
(8.8- & 9-Inch Axle ID)

Third Digit	Model & Year
A	Ford/Galaxie (1958 on)
B	Bronco (1970–73), Maverick (1975–77), Fairmount (1978–83)
C	Remanufactured Parts (1966–75), Elite (1975), Capri (1979 on)
D	Falcon (1960–69), Maverick (1970–74), Granada (1975–83), LTD (1983 on)
E	Chassis Cab Truck (1970–73), Pinto (1976–80), Escort (1981 on)
F	Export sales, Trans Am Racing
G	Comet (1961–67), Montego (1968–76), EXP (1982 on)
H	High Performance Part, Medium and Heavy Truck (1966 on)
I	Not used
J	Marine and Industrial Engines
K	Edsel (1958–60), Comet (1975–77), Zephyr (1978–83), Marquis (1983 on)
L	Lincoln (1958–60), Mark (1961 on)
M	Mercury (1958 on)
N	Tractor (1958 on)
O	Fairlane (1962–68), Torino (1969–76), LTDII (1977–79), LN7 (1982–83)
P	Autolite and 1962 on, Motorcraft Brand
Q	Not used
R	Rotunda Tools (1962–69), Ford of Europe (1970 on), Remanufactured parts (1976 on)
S	Thunderbird (1958 on)
T	Truck (1958–65), Light and Medium Truck (1966–82), Bronco (1966–70, 73–82), Light Truck and Full–Size Bronco (1983 on)
U	Econoline and Club Wagon Van (1961–81)
V	Lincoln Continental (1961–81)
W	Cougar (1967–80, 83 on), XR7 (1981–82)
X	Truck (1970–73)
Y	Meteor in Canada (1962–72), Bobcat (1975–80), Lynx (1981 on)
Z	Mustang (1964–73), Mustang II (1974–78), Mustang (1979 on)
1	Not used
2	Pinto (1972–75)
3	Tempo (1984 on)
4	Comet (1971–74), Monarch (1975–80), Cougar (1981–82), Marquis (1983 on)
5	RVs (1974–75), Continental (1982 on)
6	Pantera (1971–75), Topaz (1984 on)
7	Courier (1971–85), Ranger, Bronco II (1983 on), Explorer (1991 on)
8	Capri (1972–75)
9	Turbine Engine Parts (1970–75)

The third character in our example (C4AW-4025-B) is an A, which indicates it is from a Ford vehicle, specifically a Galaxie from 1958 or newer.

Ford Part Number Fourth Character
(8.8- & 9-Inch Axle ID)

Fourth Digit	Design Engineering Office
A	Light Truck Engineering Division
B	Body and Electrical Product Division
C	Chassis
D	Overseas Product Engineering
E	Engine North America
F	Electronics Division
G	Engine Merkenich Germany
H	Climate Control (1972 on)
I	Not used
J	Ford Parts and Customer Service Division
K	Import Release
L	Ford Customer Service Division Power Products
M	Performance and Special Vehicle Operations
N	Volvo
O	Outside
P	Transmission and Axle
Q	Diesel Engine
R	Manul Transmission
S	Light and Heavy Truck Special Order Parts
T	Electrical
U	Fuel and Handling Division
V	Domestic Special Order
W	Axle and Driveshaft
X	Plastic and Trim
Y	Special Vehicle
Z	Ford Service Parts, Product Analysis
1	European Product Development Center
2	Land Rover
3	Large and Luxury Vehicle Center
4	Truck Vehicle Center
5	South America Operations
6	Otomobil Sanayi, Turkey JV
7	Transmission and Axle
8	Hybrid and Electric Vehicle
9	Asia Pacific and Australia

So a 2011 Mustang axle is part number BR3W-4001-KH.

The last character designates which Design Engineering Office is responsible for the component. There is a fair amount of detailed information contained within the part number for Ford components.

The differential is identified by a basic part number, but you may find an engineering part number, which is usually part of the casting, and a service part number, which is found on the parts box or found in the dealer parts system. Regardless whether it is the service part number or the engineering part number, the basic number remains the same. Keep in mind that sometimes an engineering part number was placed on the casting of a part that was used on a different vehicle. So, proceed with caution with this information because it only serves as a basic indicator.

The basic part number is a series of numbers systematically developed to further divide the vehicle into sub-systems. In fact, sub-assemblies or accessory kits often had a letter in the second position of the basic number. For example, the base number for shift level is 7213 while the indicator for the shift level is 7A213. The C-washers for axle retention are 4N237, axle brackets are 4A263, and even the differential bearing shims are 4A451.

Another set of basic numbers is reserved for body components and yet another set for service tools, but

The fourth character represents the Engineering Operations area responsible for the component and to no surprise, the W in our example (C4AW-4025-B) represents Axle and Driveshaft Engineering.

we are focused on the axle and driveshaft for the purposes of this book.

The last sequence of numbers or suffix provides revision control for the Design Engineer. Typically, the first revision was given the suffix A and then sequenced to B and so on as design revisions were made. The design revisions were typically very minor, and the parts were interchangeable but of course, you wanted the latest revision. If there were significant changes, the entire part number was updated. But there are exceptions to this as well. For example, the A revision could be an intake manifold for a 2-barrel carburetor, while the B revision could be the 4-barrel carburetor version of the same engine manifold.

There is even a series of part number conventions for fasteners that references thread pitch and coatings.

Ford Part Number 1999-On
(8.8- & 9-Inch Axle ID)

Code	Year	Code	Year
X	1999	E	2014
Y	2000	F	2015
1	2001	G	2016
2	2002	H	2017
3	2003	J	2018
4	2004	K	2019
5	2005	L	2020
6	2006	M	2021
7	2007	N	2022
8	2008	P	2023
9	2009	R	2024
A	2010	S	2025
B	2011	T	2026
C	2012	V	2027
D	2013	W	2028

The 1999 model year and on follows a single-digit format. An example is EV6P, where E means 2014, V6 is the vehicle model (Escape), and P is the design responsibility within Ford and happens to be Automatic Transmission Engineering.

Ford Core Part Numbers
(8.8- & 9-Inch Axle ID)

Part Numbers	Functional Area	Part Numbers	Functional Area
1000 - 1250	Wheels, hubs, and drums	13300 - 13399	Turn signal
1251 - 1349	Not assigned	13400 - 13699	License, tail, and stop lamps
1350 - 1499	Spare wheel carrier	13700 - 13799	Courtesy, dome, and instrument lamps and switches
1500 - 1724	Tires and tubes		
1725 - 1999	Not assigned	13800 - 13949	Horn
2000 - 2874	Brakes	13950 - 13999	Not assigned
2875 - 2999	Air compressor	14000 - 14689	Wiring and circuit breakers, terminals and connectors, window regulator, and fuse panel
3000 - 3499	Front axles and front suspension		
3500 - 3776	Steering gear and steering wheel		
3777 - 3999	Not assigned	14690 - 14724	Seat regulator (electrical)
4000 - 4999	**Rear axle and driveshaft**	14725 - 14999	Junction boxes and electrical conduit
5000 - 5149	Frame and brackets	15000 - 15074	Clocks and cigar lighter
5200 - 5299	Muffler, exhaust pipe and brackets	15075 - 15114	Lamp assembly cluster
5300 - 5350	Front springs	15115 - 15199	Inactive
5351 - 5416	Sub-frame (for cab mounting)	15200 - 15399	Road and spotlamps
5417 - 5454	Not assigned	15400 - 15489	Lamp assembly marker
5455 - 5481	Front springs (clips, studs, and bushings)	15490 - 15579	Lamp assembly backup and utility
5482 - 5499	Stabilizer and attaching parts	15580 - 15599	Lamp assembly Police flasher
5500 - 5515	Front spring covers	15600 - 15649	Inactive
5516 - 5999	Rear springs and attaching parts	15650 - 15655	Map light
6000 - 6899	Engine and mounts	15656 - 15699	Top control
6900 - 6944	Inactive	15700 - 15724	Engine compartment lamp
6945 - 6999	Engine installation and dress-up kits	15725 - 15759	Commercial pump motors (not used on passenger car, truck, and industrial engines)
7000 - 7999	Transmission and clutch		
8000 - 8499	Radiator and grille parts		
8500 - 8599	Water pumps	15760 - 15799	Not assigned
8600 - 8699	Fan and brackets	15800 - 15849	Lamp assembly transmission control selector indicator
8670 - 8999	Not assigned		
9000 - 9423	Fuel tank, gauges, pumps, and lines	15850 - 15874	Parking brake signal
9424 - 9499	Manifolds, clamps, thermostats, etc.	16000 - 16299	Front fenders, aprons, and shields
9500 - 9599	Carburetor	16300 - 16449	Rear fenders
9600 - 9699	Air cleaner	16450 - 16549	Running boards and brackets
9700 - 9899	Thermostatic choke, accelerator spark, and choke control rods	16550 - 16579	Splash shields
		16580 - 16599	Not assigned
9900 - 9999	Inactive	16600 - 16999	Hood, brackets, and controls
10000 - 10399	Generators and alternators	17000 - 17149	Tools
10400 - 10499	Not assigned	17150 - 17249	Not assigned
10500 - 10649	Voltage regulator	17250 - 17384	Speedometer and tachometer
10650 - 10837	Batteries and ammeters	17385 - 17399	Not assigned
10838 - 10999	Instrument cluster and controls	17400 - 17674	Windshield wipers and washers
11000 - 11529	Starter motor and starter switch	17675 - 17748	Rearview mirrors
11530 - 11568	Not assigned	17749 - 17999	Front bumpers, rear bumpers, and stone deflectors
11569 - 11619	Ignition switch		
11620 - 11644	Not assigned	18000 - 18199	Shock absorbers
11645 - 11688	Lighting switch	18200 - 18241	Inactive
11689 - 11999	Not assigned	18242 - 18699	Heaters
12000 - 12427	Ignition coil, distributor, and spark plugs	18700 - 18799	Air brakes
12428 - 12449	Not assigned	18800 - 19499	Radio
12450 - 12499	Engine governor	19500 - 19549	Miscellaneous accessories
12500 - 12999	Not assigned	19550 - 19999	Air conditioners
13000 - 13299	Headlamps and parking lamps		

The core (or center) portion of the number provides further clarification as to the specific area of the vehicle. There are some gaps such as 5150–5199. The rear axle and driveshaft designations (bold) are in the 4000–4999 range and our example (C4AW-4025-B) of 4025 fits right in there.

AXLE REMOVAL

You have a couple of options when servicing the rear axle. You can do all the work with the axle installed in the car or remove the axle from the car and perform the work on an axle fixture. Each method has advantages and disadvantages. Are you working on a vehicle hoist or using a floor jack and jack stands? If you are planning to just perform a rebuild that requires replacing bearings and seals, then the axle can stay in the car. If you are going to shorten the axle housing, repaint, or powdercoat the axle, then you need to remove the entire axle assembly from the vehicle.

Since the disassembly process is the same for the 8.8-inch and the 9-inch, the removal process of a generic axle is covered here (see Chapter 3 for the 8.8-inch and Chapter 5 for the 9-inch axle). Chapter 8 discusses upgrading the stock axle on a 1957 Bel Air to a Ford 9-inch, so that vehicle is also used as an example in this chapter.

Safety Equipment

The most important aspect of safety is to be aware of your surroundings and take the time to remove any dangerous or hazardous items. In addition, if you have been working for too long and feel fatigued, it is best to stop and get some much-needed rest. The work can wait until the next day.

Keep in mind that many auto components are heavy and care should be taken to avoid dropping them. At times, this means that you want to use some sort of lift assist, such as a jack, or a second person. Make certain that you are using a

Prior to disassembling the entire axle, check the preload of the limited-slip differential to verify that it needs a rebuild and to get an indication of the overall condition of the axle. An excessively worn limited-slip differential helps to understand the type of usage that it has experienced. (I have made a simple fixture that is just a plate with the bolt pattern drilled into it and I welded a nut to the center. Now I can just jack one tire off the ground, with the parking brake off, and check the breakaway torque.)

Place a torque wrench on the center nut (I like to use a beam- or dial-style wrench for this) and rotate the wheel while reading the torque required to make the wheel rotate initially. Once the wheel starts turning, the torque required decreases to keep the wheel rotating. If the breakaway torque is less than 50 ft-lbs, a rebuild is in order. A typical range for a performance street car is between 110 and 140 ft-lbs.

floor jack and jack stands that are rated for your vehicle. I actually like to get the vehicle as high as possible and use large six-ton-rated jack stands, which allows more room underneath the vehicle.

I often refer to assembly grease to help hold parts together or pre-lube seals. Always make certain to use a good Type-2 grease, which is readily available at most parts stores. It is also a good idea to have a supply of brake cleaner, RTV, and thread locker.

Always wear the correct eye protection, clothing, and shoes. Remove all jewelry and tie back long hair before performing any service work. If any cutting torches or welding work is required, use the correct eye shields and remove any solvents or dirty rags that may be in the area.

Always have a fire extinguisher that is up to date and nearby, just in case. There are four classes of fire extinguishers: Class A is for general combustibles such as paper, wood, and cloth. Class B is for flammable liquids and greases such as gasoline, oil thinners, and solvents. Class C is for electrical fires. Class D is for combustible metals such as powdered aluminum, sodium, or magnesium. There are also "combination" extinguishers that are rated for several classes. Be sure to have the right type of fire extinguisher for the components you're working on.

Gear oil, especially used oil, is very stimulating to your sense of smell, or in other words it stinks very badly. If it gets on my clothes, I typically end up just tossing them in the trash and don't risk putting them in the washing machine. I also like to wear disposable nitrile or similar gloves to make hand cleanup easier and to avoid getting the smelly and oftentimes burned oil on my hands. Once it gets on your hands, it can take days to wear off.

I show some of my homemade specialty tools and purchased tools that are unique and not typically found in the standard mechanic's toolbox. Some of these are special bearing pullers, pinion flange holding equipment, precision dial indicator, inch-pound torque wrenches, and seal pullers.

Finally, a very important aspect of safety is to keep your work area clean and uncluttered.

General Procedures

The first step is to get the vehicle in the air. If you do not have access to a hoist (I didn't), jack up the vehicle as high as possible and put jack stands under the frame. This allows the axle to drop freely.

Typically, the shocks are the travel limiters of the axle at full rebound. So, once the vehicle is securely supported by jack stands, remove the shocks. This allows the axle assembly to drop even lower in the chassis. Without the shocks attached, the axle lowers farther, so you can closely inspect the exhaust and brake lines and cables to make certain that they are not the travel limiters. On some vehicles, the brake cables or hoses may have to be removed to allow the axle to drop freely. This is the reason that you want to have the car chassis as high as possible—to allow for this extra travel.

The Tri-Five (1955–1957 Chevrolet passenger car) rear shock arrangement uses an upper shock mount that is accessed from inside the trunk. This upper shock mount arrangement will be replaced with an additional frame crossmember (see Chapter 8).

With the top mounts removed, the lower mounts can be removed next.

I also noticed while underneath the vehicle that the dual exhaust tailpipes had an interesting routing path. When you purchase a classic car that has had multiple owners, the total number of previous repairs and quality of the workmanship over the life of the vehicle can be questionable. Take your time and look things over carefully before you purchase any used vehicle.

With the rear shocks removed, I can turn my attention to removing the driveshaft. Most driveshafts are bolted to the axle pinion flange and just need to be unbolted.

Tri-Five vehicles use a leaf spring style (or Hotchkis) of rear suspension. If your vehicle has a coil-style arrangement, there are some differences for removing the axle from the vehicle. The main one is that there are control arms bolted between the axle and frame or body that need to be removed.

Before beginning the leaf spring removal, remove the brake lines and cables to get them out of the way. This is probably the biggest deterrent to most owners when removing an axle as the brake lines may be excessively corroded and the head of the brake fitting may strip. The parking brake cables may require you to disassemble the brake hardware and shoes to release the cable from within the backing plates. Also, when you re-install the axle, bleed the hydraulic brake system to remove any air from the lines. Make sure that the bleeder screws on the wheel cylinders (if you have drums) or calipers (if you have discs) are not rusted in place before you get to that step.

Once the vehicle has been properly supported, remove the wheels and tires. This is the original axle for this vehicle, which has been sitting in a barn since 1972. The axle has rusted over time, and therefore it has plenty of rusted, stubborn fasteners. One of the wheel studs has already been broken off because it was severely rusted and difficult to remove, which is common on used units. Some folks are afraid of the simple process of pressing a new stud in place and leave a unit just like this.

To replace the stud, just drive the old stud out of the flange with a hammer and punch. With the correct stud for the application it simply installs from the back of the flange and the knurled surface is pressed in place. If this is going to be performed with the axle shaft still in the axle, use a nut with a few well-lubed washers along with oil on the stud threads to pull the stud in place.

Brake System Removal

Professional Mechanic Tip

1 Remove Shock Stud

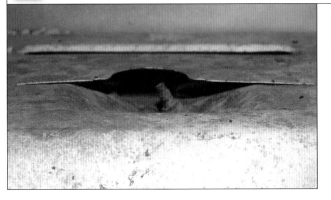

Here you can see the upper shock stud with nut in place just below the back of the rear seat. Typically, a couple of flats are machined into the top of the stud to allow you to grab the stud and keep it from turning while you remove the nut.

If you are installing a fresh set of shocks, you do not need to salvage the threads. Breaking off the stud is a way to remove shocks. Just put a deep well socket on the nut with a long extension in place. Then bend the stud back and forth a few times until it is fatigued and breaks off.

Professional Mechanic Tip

2 Remove Shock Mount

The lower shock mounts are located on a stud that is welded to the leaf spring mounting bracket. Some axles have the lower shock mount welded to the axle itself. This one shows its age with the amount of rust and bushing deterioration. Unfortunately, I ended up breaking off one of the studs during the removal process. Penetrating oil is the first step for removing rusty fasteners, and when all else fails, use heat from a torch. (See Chapter 8 for stud repair.)

3 Inspect Brake Line Routing

Here you can see the shock with the flex hose for the rear brake just in front of it. Notice how the exhaust was routed underneath the brake hose and the hose actually rests on the hot exhaust. This is a perfect example of how not to route an exhaust system. This is an accident just waiting to happen.

4 Inspect Parking Brake Cable Routing

 Upon further inspection, I noticed that the parking brake cable was in contact with both exhaust pipes.

5 Remove Strap Nuts

Having a strong coat of oil on the axle pinion seal along with the engine and transmission is fortuitous because the oil on the front of the axle significantly inhibits rust. This axle is a grimy mess from years of oil leaking and road debris sticking to it, but fortunately it hasn't rusted. Here you can see the typical GM strap–style universal joint retention. There are just four nuts that hold the two straps in place. You can also see the driveshaft's welded-on balance weight, a couple inches forward of the U-joint strap.

Remove all four nuts from the straps. Then lightly pry the driveshaft forward and remove it from the axle. This vehicle has a slip at the transmission output-style driveshaft, which is typical for most muscle cars. Once you have the driveshaft clear of the pinion flange, pull it out of the transmission and set it aside. Place a drop pan underneath the driveshaft so you're prepared to catch a small amount of transmission fluid that leaks out of the transmission.

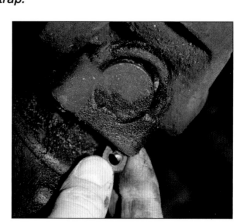

You may have to push the strap partially out of the yoke. These nuts can be a little tricky to access; use a box-end wrench because there is not enough room for a socket and ratchet. It is possible to use a socket with a swivel and extension arrangement on some applications.

6 Remove Cable

The parking brake cable runs through an equalizer bar underneath the car. You just need to pull back the protective dirt boot and remove the retaining clip to the frame bracket. The U-shaped retaining clip has a bent-over tab on the closed end. You can grab this tab with pliers or even tap it with a large-tip screwdriver to remove it. Once the clip has been removed, push the cable housing out of the bracket. There is a slot in the bracket that allows the cable to come free once the cable housing is removed.

Repeat this procedure for the other side and then slip the cable out of the center equalizer bracket. (I am not disconnecting the cable from the brakes as I am going to replace this entire axle with a disc brake arrangement with all new cables.)

7 Remove Hydraulic Line

The flexible hydraulic line is the last piece of the brake system that needs to be removed. A bracket is welded to the axle housing that supports the junction block for the brake lines to the individual wheels. This bracket also has an anti-rotation feature, so it's easy to remove the flexible line. Be sure to clean off the crud and use the correct-size line wrench to remove the brake hose. You need to be careful as brake fluid leaks out when this line is removed. Brake fluid removes paint and damages most surfaces, so be careful as you catch the fluid, and don't let it get all over your shop.

Leaf Spring Removal

1 Remove Fasteners

If your leaf springs have never been removed from the car, it's not going to be easy. Soak them with penetrating oil for a few hours. If that doesn't help you may need to resort to heating the bolts with a methylacetylene propadiene (MAPP) gas torch to break them loose. Always be careful when heating the fasteners as any residual penetrating fluid may catch on fire. It is a good idea to clean all of the penetrant off and never spray penetrant or any fluid on the fastener after it has been heated and is still hot.

Using MAPP gas or the equivalent, evenly apply heat to the entire nut and circulate the torch around the fastener to achieve even heating for at least 30 to 60 seconds and then try to loosen the fastener. If the nut is still stuck, apply heat for an additional 30 seconds and try again. If all else fails, keep applying heat until the nut is red hot; it should loosen then.

Here, you can see that the second spring in the spring pack appears to have a sharp square end. The spring end actually broke off.

2 Inspect Rear Suspension

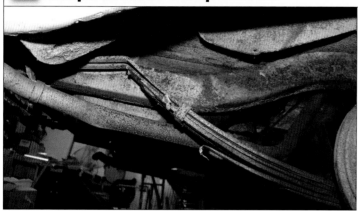

This car sits very low in the rear, and this certainly isn't the stock ride height. The previous owner lowered the car and decided to use a torch to heat the springs until the car sank the required amount. The V-shape in the top leaf is not a production design; rather, it is from the torch action. The second leaf was even cut off to further allow the top leaf to flatten out and the rear suspension to lower. This is another perfect example of how not to perform a task on your car, such as lowering.

Professional Mechanic Tip

3 Remove Leaf Spring Nuts

Long U-shaped bolts fasten the leaf spring pack to the axle. There are a couple options to remove them. You can just turn the nuts until the U-bolts break or you can try to save the nuts.

To save the nuts, heat them with MAPP gas, which produces a much hotter flame when compared to traditional propane. It usually comes in yellow containers as compared to the blue propane containers and is available at most hardware stores. MAPP gas is more convenient to use than oxyacetylene.

Evenly apply heat around the nut until it turns red hot. This typically takes a minute or so; while the nut is still hot, try to loosen it. If the nut is still stuck in place, continue to apply heat until it loosens. Once the nut begins to loosen, make certain to completely remove it or otherwise, as it cools, it may shrink and seize in place again.

4 Remove Leaf Spring Shackle Bolts

Leaf spring shackle bolts probably don't want to come apart either. You can use heat to help get the fasteners off. Then pry the shackles off. My bushings were ruined from the heat, but I have to replace the leaf springs anyway. (See Chapter 8 for more on spring shackle brackets.)

5 Remove Spring

Once the outer shackle is out of the way, pry the spring off the stud. These springs may be corroded in place and need some extra effort to get them out of the vehicle. Be careful and make sure that the axle is supported when you are removing the springs, as they should be the last piece that is holding the axle in the car.

6 Inspect Vent Hole

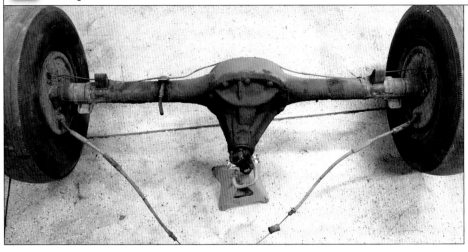

After you remove the axle, keep the parking brake cables in place. Also leave the wheels and tires on to make it easier to move around the shop without the aid of a jack or second person. Inspect the vent hole on the driver-side axle tube.

I discovered someone had removed the vent cap and never replaced it, so this axle was leaking fluid out the vent, and road debris and water was entering the axle—another reason to replace the entire axle.

7 Clean Vent Hole

If your axle will be completely disassembled and thoroughly cleaned, use a wire brush to remove any vent hole debris. Of course, some of this debris may fall in the hole but you can clean it out later.

Note that the jounce bumper mounts to the axle, and a small tab is welded on top of the axle to help locate the bracket. The other side of the bracket is held in place under the U-bolt. The U-bolt mounting pads are on the bottom of the axle tubes and the leaf spring pack goes underneath the axle. As a result, this is called an underslung-style mounting arrangement. Some axles have the leaf spring mounted on top of the tubes and are called overslung.

This is the brake junction block mounting bracket. The mounting hole is an oval shape that keeps the block from rotating. You can also see the tab for the jounce bumper bracket to the right of the brake line bracket.

8.8-INCH AXLE DISASSEMBLY AND INSPECTION

In 1983 the Ford 8.8-inch axle first appeared in a Ford Ranger truck, but since then, the 8.8 has been most commonly installed in the Mustang. Of course, you want your Mustang to perform at its best and have maximum longevity. Therefore, if you're building 700-hp street car or 10-second quarter-mile car, you're either going to perform a high-performance build of an 8.8-inch axle or you're going to replace the axle completely with a larger, stronger 9-inch unit. People have been saying for years that you just need to put a 9-inch axle in your car, and that's certainly an option, but it's not your only option.

This chapter reviews the steps required to fully disassemble an 8.8-inch axle and some common areas to inspect for wear. Specific details for Mustangs (but not all of the years) are also reviewed. The general steps apply to all axles even if you are working on an F-150 axle.

Optional Upgrades

The 8.8-inch can certainly be used for high-performance and racing applications, so there are good reasons to stick with the factory 8.8-inch axle, but if you do you should make some upgrades.

Axle Shaft

If you are running sticky slicks and a manual transmission, both of these cause severe stress on the drivetrain, and care should be taken with them. Upgrading to 31-tooth-spline axle shafts is a must for any high-performance build because they are significantly stronger. In fact, the 31-tooth-spline axle shafts provide about a 30-percent increase in strength over the 28-tooth parts.

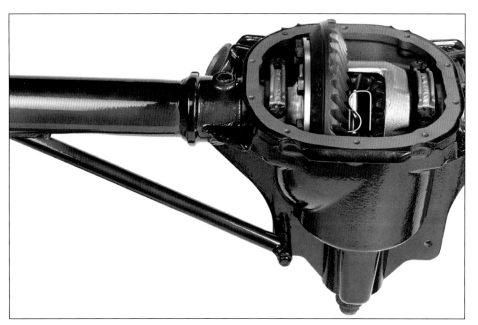

This is a complete 8.8-inch axle with the rear cover removed. The S-shaped limited-slip clutch preload spring is visible in the center of the differential. This chapter covers the removal of the differential, gears, and bearings, plus the entire disassembly and a comprehensive inspection.

Lug Pattern

While you are ordering new axles, it is a great time to upgrade from the four-lug hub to the five-lug wheel pattern to add more strength to the axle assembly. Of course, you are running sticky tires for a reason: to apply gobs of horsepower to the ground and avoid wheel spin. With a manual transmission and said sticky tires, you need a strong rear axle. Typically the axle shaft fails first in the low-400-hp range and with repeated drag strip launches.

Caliper Brackets

When the axle shaft fails on a C-washer-style axle, such as the 8.8 axle, nothing is holding the wheel in place, except for the disc brake caliper brackets, if your vehicle has rear discs. These brackets were never designed to withstand axle failures and this high level of loading, and therefore they end up failing as well. Consequently, the National Hot Rod Association (NHRA) rules call for C-clip eliminators for car running 10.99-second or faster ETs. The real robust fix is to have the 9-inch style, 3/4-float-style wheel end bearing arrangement welded to the 8.8-inch axle housing. Most aftermarket rebuilders, such as Strange, Moser, and Currie, can perform this high-performance upgrade. You just need to send them the axle.

Automatic Transmission

The automatic transmission offers some protection depending on whether there is a manual valve body and transmission brake installed. Typically, automatic cars do not start snapping axle shafts until 550 or more horsepower is produced. Keep in mind that the differential is next as the weak link, and it can fail before the axle shafts. It is good insurance to use a housing brace and rear-cover girdle at these power levels. When the power exceeds 600 hp and with good traction, the actual housing itself and tubes tend to bend. At this point, it is time to upgrade to the stronger and heavier 9-inch axle. Some owners used the 8.8-inch axle in high-horsepower applications, but the driver has to be careful not to bend the axle and smoothly apply the power, which is not always possible when drag racing but works in other types of racing.

Pinion Spacer

If the axle is going to be abused, it is also a great upgrade to replace the collapsible pinion spacer with a solid spacer kit from manufacturers such as Ratech.

Driveshaft and U-Joints

In addition the driveshaft and U-joints should be upgraded. A good upgrade is to go to the stronger 1350-style flanges and universal joints.

Disassembly Preparation

The first step is to get the vehicle raised in the air as high as possible. Larger six-ton jack stands are recommended to support the vehicle by the subframe. This allows the axle to hang as low as possible and gives more room to work underneath the vehicle. If you have a hoist, then you have plenty of room. Depending on

Professional Mechanic Tip

1 Jack Up Car

First, place a hydraulic floor jack on the center section of the axle just forward of the cover flange and then jack up the vehicle. Do not apply any load to the cover itself; doing so may damage it. Some of the 8.8-inch axles had plastic covers (typically found on the Ford Rangers) and you can damage the cover by placing the jack on it. Also, the vibration damper is installed on the axle just in front of the jack. It is a cast-iron weight that straddles the pinion area of the axle housing. Keep in mind that this damper can get in the way of the fill plug on some vehicles. Securely support the car on jack stands.

Remove the wheels and brake drums or calipers as required. If you have a disc-brake arrangement, you never want to let the calipers just hang from the flex hoses. Use zip ties or mechanic's wire to hold them out of the way. Also, mark where the driveshaft flange connects to the axle flange so you can return them to the same orientation to avoid any potential vibration issues later. Once they are both marked remove the driveshaft.

2 Remove Axle Cover

Securely support the car on the jack stands or hoist. The next step is to position a drip pan under the center of the axle, and remove the rear cover. Remove the 10 cover bolts with a standard socket and ratchet and then gently pry off the cover. I like to leave a bolt or two toward the top of the cover still in place but loosened. This allows me to pry off the cover, but not have it pop right off. This avoids some of the potential mess from the gear oil pouring all over the shop floor. Once the cover has been partially removed the oil flows out (shown). Used gear oil, and especially burned gear oil, is very smelly stuff. So make sure that you have plenty of ventilation and get the old oil into a sealed container for proper recycling.

3 Inspect Differential Assembly

With the cover removed, inspect the axle internals. This Traction-Lok differential is based on the clutch pack and S-shaped preload spring. You can also see that this axle has been serviced before; the telltale sign is that the original assembly plant did not use blue RTV sealant but rather black.

the amount of work you are going to perform, it may make sense to pull the entire axle from the vehicle, especially if you are going to paint the axle.

Make certain that you have plenty of room on either side of the vehicle to remove the axle shafts. A typical single-car garage may be tight. The axle shafts need to clear the axle housing to be fully removed.

If you are going to perform a standard rebuild, which means replacing bearings, seals, and clutch pack, it is imperative to take good notes of the shims' locations so you can return the axle back into service with minimal adjustments required. It has been rare that I have opened up an axle that did not need some replacement parts besides just the common

wear items like bearings and seals so be prepared for a few surprises.

Axle Housing Disassembly

The 8.8-inch axle can be found on many different vehicles, with the Mustang being the most common. It can also be found on any of the smaller trucks with the 4.0-liter V-6 engine, such as the Explorer, Mountaineer, Ranger, and even the Aerostar. Some F-150s and Econoline vans with a V-6 engine also come with the 8.8-inch axle in the rear. Even some late-1990s trucks with the 4.6-liter V-8 engine used this axle.

The four-wheel-drive F-Series, Expedition, and Navigator use a special version of the 8.8-inch on the front

axle. This particular differential is an aluminum, independent suspension arrangement with an opposite-hand spiral angle on the gears (commonly

Face-Hobbed Gear Set

If you notice that the beveled outer surface of the ring gear is left un-machined and as-forged, it is a visual telltale sign that it is a Ford original face-hobbed gear set. The face-milled gears have this surface machined, which is important when it is time to set the correct gear pattern position (see Chapter 7 for more detail). ∎

1 Measure Shaft Runout

 Depending on your rebuild plan, it may make sense to verify axle shaft runout by setting up a dial indicator. The dial indicator base has a magnetic portion that is mounted to the brake backing plate. Then the dial indicator stand portion is adjusted in order to achieve the correct position of the dial pointer. You can also remove the axle shaft and support it on V-blocks. (If you are simply upgrading the axle shafts, there is no reason to take these measurements.)

Push the axle shaft inboard as far as possible until it contacts the differential pin. Rotate the shaft while observing the needle on the dial indicator. Be careful when rotating the shaft that the shaft does not plunge in or out. If it does, it artificially increases the runout values. Per Ford's specifications, the axle shaft runout should not exceed .030 inch.

If the shaft is out of specification, always replace it. Never attempt to straighten the shaft or flange because it will prematurely fatigue and break. The axle shaft holds the wheel on the vehicle for a semi-float axle arrangement such as the 8.8-inch. If you are upgrading shafts and the differential for any performance type of build, go with the stronger 31-tooth spline axles.

2 Remove Retention Bolt

To remove the axle shafts from the axle housing, remove the C-washers that are retaining the axle shafts. In order to gain access, remove the differential pin-retention bolt, along with the differential pin. The axle shafts are then free to be pushed inward for access to the C-washer. Remove the differential pin-retention bolt and the differential.

Here, I have rotated the differential so that the differential pin is accessible. It is kind of tricky to get a socket on it. A closed-end wrench fits on the fastener head but it is typically too short to provide enough leverage to loosen the bolt. I have an 8-mm, 6-point, 3/8-inch-drive socket in my toolbox just for this situation. The retention bolt is partially removed in the photo.

3 Remove Differential Pin

The differential pin should slide out easily. If the differential pin and pinion bores have excessive wear, there may be a slight step worn in the differential pin. If this is the case, the pin is very difficult to remove. Unfortunately, there is no way to continue the disassembly process if the pin cannot be removed. If the pin shows extreme wear, you may have to cut the pin in order to remove it. (I have had to resort to using a plasma cutter on a couple of occasions to cut the differential pin and housing into pieces to get them out. These were units that actually had a pinion gear fail, causing excessive wear on the pin.) This pin shows signs of typical wear and can safely be re-used. You can see the two oval-shaped witness marks near the center of the pin, which are typical from the axle shaft banging into the pin during cornering maneuvers. This is common and nothing to be concerned about.

4 Remove Drum or Disc Brakes

The typical disc brake setup has the caliper still in place (left). In some instances the rotors or drums are rusted tight and cannot be easily removed. If this is what you find, use a mallet to hit the drum or rotor between the wheel studs and drive it back on the shaft to break the rust loose. Be careful not to hit the wheel studs or you could damage the threads. This sometimes works. In a worst case scenario (right) you may need to resort to an oxyacetylene torch for help. Using a torch is a last resort, as this will surely damage any speed sensors that are behind the rotor. (I am not too worried about damaging the axle seals as I always replace them as a matter of practice.) If this doesn't work, there are special pullers that can be used to apply pressure to remove the drum or disc.

If all else fails, the drum may need to be cut in half with an angle grinder. This method is a messy, noisy, and time-consuming process and care needs to be taken to not cut into any of the brake hardware that is underneath the drum.

5 Remove Wheel Sensors

On most modern Mustang axles, the anti-lock brake system (ABS) tone wheel and wheel sensor is located on the axle shaft, and this needs to be removed. The ABS debuted on the SN95 model in the 1994 model year. Some of the earlier axles have it trapped between the ring gear and differential case, while pre-ABS units do not have them at all. The engineer in me hates this design because the speed sensor needs to be removed and is easily damaged during removal.

To remove the sensor, push the axle shaft in far enough to gain access to the C-washer. An inverted Torx-headed bolt holds the sensor from the back side of the plating with perfect access. The correct socket with a 1/4-inch-drive ratchet is adequate to loosen and remove the bolt. Corrosion typically builds up on the sensor, and there is no easy way to apply load to it to remove the sensor. I usually end up with a 50/50 chance of damaging the sensors. Replacement sensors are readily available at a local parts store or Ford dealership.

6 Remove C-Washer

Once everything is clear on the wheel end side and the differential pin has been removed, push the axle shafts inward with your hands to gain access to the c-washer that holds the axle shaft in place. The axle shaft should slide inward easily and not require excessive force. If excessive force is required, this is a sign that the axle shaft or housing may be bent.

6 Remove C-Washer CONTINUED

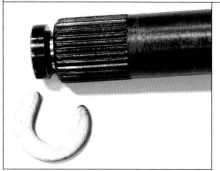

I have had to resort to a large hammer to drive a severely bent axle shaft inward but this is a rare and damaged unit. It is a gold-colored washer and slotted to allow it to match the groove in the end of the axle shaft to allow for assembly and disassembly of the unit. This washer can be a little tricky to get to and, with the gear oil and O-ring on the axle shaft, difficult to get loose.

Use a small flathead screwdriver (page 34) to partially push it off the axle shaft and then use a magnetic pick-up tool to pull it out. Repeat this procedure for the other side of the axle shaft as well. The axle shaft groove and C-washer are shown at left.

Critical Inspection

7 Remove Axle Shaft from Housing

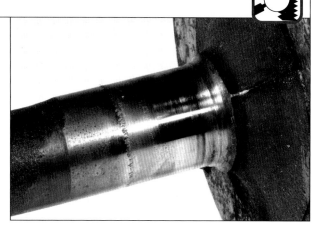

I always recommend replacing the wheel end seals; use two hands to guide the axle shaft out of the housing (left). Use a shop towel to help catch and strip off some of the gear oil as the shaft is being removed. Once the axle shaft has been removed, closely inspect the wheel end bearing surface as the axle shaft is the bearing inner race. This area often shows signs of wear, surface pitting, and frosting. This shaft and bearing probably made a growling noise in the vehicle that increased with speed (right). It needs to be replaced.

8 Remove Wheel End Seal and Bearings

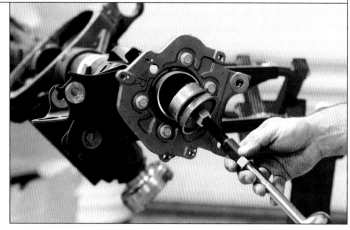

With a bearing puller tool (left) and slide hammer, use a half dozen or so hits with the slide hammer puller to remove the bearing and seal (right). This example has a pivoting foot at the end that goes in behind the bearing. Once the foot has been placed behind the bearing, reach in and align it, so it is perpendicular to the bearing.

9 Remove Differential

Unbolt the bearing caps and remove them, making certain to keep track of their location. They will be re-installed in their original location and cannot be swapped from side to side or installed upside down. They are machined with the axle housing and are a matched set to the housing locations. Mark them and the axle housing immediately with two little center-punch marks on the seal surface at about 3 o'clock. Also mark the caps.

The bearings and shims feature a factory interference fit on the differential assembly. The bearings should be a tight fit, but if there's been a substantial amount of wear, they may be not be tight. To overcome this tight fit, place a large screwdriver on the housing and into the differential pin hole. Use a pry bar between the housing and one of the ring gear bolts. The differential with the ring gear installed is very heavy and you don't want this to fall out, hit the shop floor, or hit any part of your body. If it does, serious injury to the differential or yourself could result. Also, never pry on the ring gear teeth as you will most certainly damage the tooth surface and ruin the gear.

As the differential comes out of the axle housing, make certain to keep track of the cast-iron shims and which side that they came out of. You should bag and tag these parts to aid in reassembly. If for some reason one or both are cracked, just make certain to measure the thickness. I have used cracked shims in the past as they only act as spacers, but it depends on the amount of damage to the shim.

10 Remove Propshaft Flange

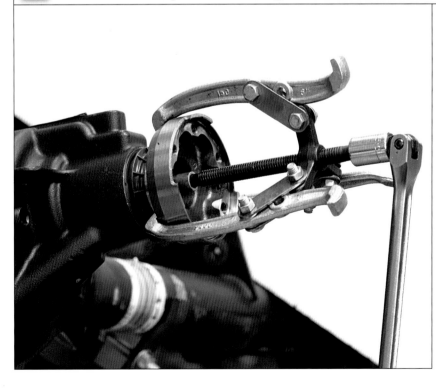

With the differential and bearings out, the pinion gear and bearings are the last items to remove. Newer Mustangs have a constant-velocity flange on the rear propshaft joint. With the independent type of flange, the spline on the pinion shaft has a slight helix, or twist, in the spline to remove any potential source of backlash or clonk from the inter-face. This is great but makes difficult work to remove and install the flange. Remove the pinion nut and use an impact gun to remove the gear. (See Chapter 4 for details about a flange-holding tool for reassembly.) A typical three-jaw puller works perfect to remove the flange. Once the flange has been removed, the pinion can be pushed out the back of the axle housing. The pinion comes out with the head bearing still pressed on, plus the col-lapsible spacer.

11 Pry Out Pinion Seal

The last parts still in the housing are the pinion seal, oil slinger, tail bearing, and races. The pinion seal just needs to be pried out with a seal remover tool; even a large screwdriver or pry bar suffices. Take special care to make sure you are prying on just the seal can and not the oil slinger behind it. The oil slinger needs to be re-used and you don't want to bend or damage it.

12 Identify Oil Slinger

Once the seal is out, you can see the oil slinger and tail bearing. The only part that is going to be re-used is the oil slinger.

13 Remove Pinion Head Bearing

Use a typical bearing spreader tool (above) to remove the pinion head bearing (right). I am not going to re-use the bearing but want to gain access to the shim that is behind it. This will be important during the re-assembly process (see Chapter 4). Make certain that the tool is grabbing the back side of the bearing race and not the cage. If you remove the bearing by pulling on the cage, the bearing will be ruined. Even though I am going to replace the bearing, if the bearing is in decent shape, I can open up the inside diameter with a die grinder and make this a set-up bearing for the installation process. The picture on the right shows the pinion with the bearing removed and the shim on the shaft.

Special Tool

A clamshell-style tool can be used to remove the pinion head bearing. It's a valuable tool because there is little chance of damaging the bearing. Of course, this tool is in the $400 range but can be used for the differential case bearings as well. If you are careful with a bearing spreader tool, you can do it without this tool.

14 Clean Inside of Housing

The axle housing is completely empty now, except for the pinion bearing races. Drive them out with a steel punch. Place the end of the punch on the exposed lip of the bearing race and firmly tap and move the punch around the race.

(This housing has two cutouts machined into the casting at the 3 and 9 o'clock positions to allow for access of the punch. Just keep alternating between the two sides to drive the race out.)

Once the pinion bearing races have been removed from the housing, start cleaning the internal housing. Use cans of brake cleaner and fresh shop rags. In this picture you can see the pinion bearing feed port above the pinion bearing races and the return port below the races. A fair amount of metal debris and crud tends to pile up in this area, so make sure it is clean. Spray generous amounts of solvent down the axle tubes and push rags from the wheel end side to the inside of the axle housing until they come clean. The axle shaft or a broom handle works well as the pusher.

This is what the housing looks like with the pinion bearing races removed. Use plenty of brake cleaner to remove all of the debris. Always finish with a rinse of brake cleaner to remove any pieces of shop towel.

known as reverse-cut gears). The normal spiral angle for standard rear axle gears is a left-hand spiral angle on the pinion mating with a right-hand spiral on the ring gear. These are just switched for the reverse-cut gears, so there is a right-hand spiral on the pinion mating with a left-hand spiral on the ring gear.

There are other cars that used the 8.8-inch axle as well, including Thunderbirds and Cougars with the 4.6- or the 3.9-liter engine with the 4R70W or manual transmission. The automatic overdrive (AOD) transmission cars typically received the smaller 7.5-inch rear axle. The Lincoln Mark VIII, Crown Victoria, Grand Marquis, and Town Car was equipped with the 8.8-inch axles.

With all of these different vehicles and engine/transmission combinations available, you are bound to run across many different axle variants. As with all Ford axles, the differentials and gear sets can be swapped among any of these axle housings, with the only exception being the four-wheel-drive reverse-cut front axles.

Traction-Lok Differential Disassembly

With all of the main axle housing parts disassembled, disassembly of the limited-slip differential is next. If an upgrade to a 31-tooth limited-slip or aftermarket differential is in the budget, taking the old factory unit apart can be skipped.

Depending on the mileage and wear on the axle, it may make more sense to just replace the entire unit. Excessive wear on the internal components, such as the pinion gear

bores, differential pin, and even the bevel gears, may warrant a replacement of the entire differential.

I have decided that I am going to disassemble the differential, thoroughly clean the parts, and inspect them for wear. One caveat: Never clean the clutch plates in any type of solvent-based cleaner as this may damage the resins that bond the friction material to the plates. This solvent may also soak into the friction material and change its properties to the point of the material no longer functioning correctly.

Always replace the clutch pack unless the friction plates look great. After all, the main reason for servicing the axle is to replace bearings and seals. For any performance build, carbon friction material is recommended (see Chapter 4 for more detail).

Critical Inspection

1 Remove Ring Gear

During the rebuilding process, be sure to perform a thorough inspection. Always wear safety glasses during. You need to take the differential apart and clean and inspect the pieces.

First, remove the ring gear, which is press-fit onto the differential case. Stand the differential on end on a block of wood and remove all of the ring gear bolts. Once these bolts have been removed, drive the gear off by using a punch in the bottom of the ring gear bolt holes. Alternate in a crisscross pattern to evenly remove the gear.

Never hit the gear back face or teeth directly with a hammer because damage will occur, which could cause runout on the ring gear. Also, don't hit partially engaged bolts, as you will damage the threads in the gear. I have seen many ring gears with dents on the back face and bolt threads that are damaged from these tactics.

2 Remove Preload Spring

Use a soft punch and a hammer to drive the preload spring partially out of the differential. A soft punch helps avoid any nicks or damage to the spring. Just make sure that the punch is squarely on the spring and alternate the taps until it starts to come out.

Professional Mechanic Tip

3 Drive S-Spring from Housing

Use a hammer and punch to drive the S-spring out of the housing, but keep in mind that the spring is under pressure. As it is driven out of the housing, it follows the side gear angled profile. Once it clears the housing, the spring releases its latent energy and can become a flying projectile. Be careful. To prevent the spring from flying out of place, put a shop rag on it. With the shop rag in place, you can easily continue to tap it out.

4 Remove Side Gears

If the clutch pack is worn, as most used units are, you can easily rotate the differential pinion gears by hand so they spin out of the differential case. This can be achieved with your bare hands and no special tools if the unit is worn (left). In some cases, the clutch pack is still tight and requires the use of tools for removal. I made such a tool (middle) using a piece of an old shaft welded to a chunk of steel to hold it vertical in my bench vise. Now I just set the dif-ferential over the spline, engage it with the side gear spline, and twist the differential housing. This makes quick work of spinning the pinion gears out of the differential. If the correct spline is not part of this homemade tool, I just use the original axle shaft, bolt it to a wheel, and stand it on end (right).

5 Remove Pinions from Housing

As the pinions rotate in the differential case, they align with the open windows and can be easily removed. Hold the top side gear in place as you removed the pinions. You want to avoid the side gear just falling out. Also, double-check to make sure that you have removed the pinion thrust washer. At times, it tends to stick in the differential case from a thin layer of gear oil. If this is the case, just reach in and pull out the washer.

Documentation Required

6 Remove Entire Clutch Pack and Side Gears

With the pinions out of the way, nothing is holding the side gears and clutch pack in place. As with pinions, always double-check to make sure that you have the entire clutch pack, including the shim, out of the differential case. If you are going to re-use the clutch pack (which I rarely do), keep them in the order and on which side they were removed from: ring gear flange side or passenger side.

Wipe down the plates with a rag but never use any type of solvent or cleaning solution on the plates as it is absorbed into the clutch material and contaminates it.

These clutch packs are prone to wear out and I always replace them, unless in a very rare case they are within specifics for wear. (See Chapter 4 for the correct order of friction and reaction plates.)

All of these parts have been removed from a Traction-Lok differential. For visual identification, the clutch plates are together and the pinion washers are still loosely in place. If during the axle disassembly process, the differential pin shows any signs of wear, chances are the pinion bores are worn and everything should be replaced.

A new replacement carbon fiber, 31-tooth-spline Traction-Lok (PN M-4204-F318C), can be purchased from any Ford dealership or motorsports distributor for about $280. Ford previously carried a paper-plate version (PN M-4204-F318) for the 31-tooth spline for about $260. Although it is has been discontinued, I have found some dealers still have stock. The 28-tooth version (PN M-4204-F288) has also been discontinued, although some dealers still have stock. The clutch pack kit for paper (PN M-4700-B) and for carbon fiber plates (PN M-4700-C) are available.

You also need two bottles of friction modifier; one for soaking the new plates and one for filling the axle. If the parts are in good condition, just clean the gears in solvent, check the pinion washers for wear (they should be .030 to .032 inch thick and not have any signs of grooves or wear marks), and clean up the differential case.

Always inspect the differential case after cleaning for any signs of grooves in the machined pockets where the gear washers locate or in the differential pin bores.

8.8-INCH AXLE ASSEMBLY

Axle assembly, as with any automotive assembly, is best completed if you take your time and have all of the parts clean and set out with plenty of space to work. I have found that if something doesn't seem correct, chances are it is not. If all else fails, walk away from the project and come back to it in a day or so. If this is your first axle project or you do not work on axles often, having everything neat and organized really makes the work go that much easier.

The following steps detail the assembly of a Traction-Lok-style differential and complete axle assembly. The process is very similar for an open differential, except that the clutch pack and preload spring are not required. The 8.8 axle assembly is similar to the 9-inch axle (see Chapter 6), but there are certain aspects that are unique to each.

Here are the internal components for the center portion of the axle with the exception of the wheel end bearings and seals. The axle cover is in the upper right with the pinion and flange below it. The pinion bearings, shims, and collapsible space are below that. The ring gear and bolts are at the lower left resting on the complete limited-slip differential with bearing cones installed. The remaining pieces are the differential bearing cups, shims, and the axle shaft C-washers. The limited-slip differential sub-assembly is already pre-assembled.

Traction-Lok Differential Assembly

In slippery road conditions, an open differential sends the torque to the wheel with the least amount of resistance and therefore traction is limited. You have probably experienced the single-wheel burnout.

The easiest way to check if you have a limited-slip differential and if it is still somewhat functioning is to jack the rear wheels off the ground. With the transmission in park, rotate one tire forward and watch the direction of the other tire. If it spins in the same direction, then you have a limited-slip differential. If it spins in the opposite direction, you have an open differential or a worn-out limited-slip unit.

Professional Mechanic Tip

1 Pre-Lube Clutch Plate Kit

Before assembling the differential, soak the friction plates in friction modifier for at least 30 minutes and ideally overnight. Make sure not to stack them so they are properly coated. This soaking process helps prevent the new clutch pack from chattering after assembly. I am installing the carbon fiber clutch plates that were first available on the 2003–2004 Cobra Mustangs and then the 2005–2013 GTs along with 2007-on GT500s.

You can purchase a Ford Racing rebuild kit (PN M-4700-C) that includes six carbon friction plates, eight steel reaction plates, two shims, preload spring, and differential pin-retention bolt for about $115. It features a clutch plate pack that is premeasured and has the correct shims, which takes the measuring and guesswork out of the process. I highly recommend purchasing this new clutch plate kit for your performance rebuild.

2 Purchase Friction Modifier

Important!

Always use the correct friction modifier. The Ford friction modifier can be purchased from a local Ford dealer or performance parts shops, such as Summit Racing or Jegs. The modifier also helps to hold the plates together during the assembly process. One important note here: If you are using a new pre-shimmed clutch pack, do not mix up the plates and shims. They must be kept together to ensure the correct clutch plate stack thickness. Soak the plates in a container.

3 Arrange Clutch Pack

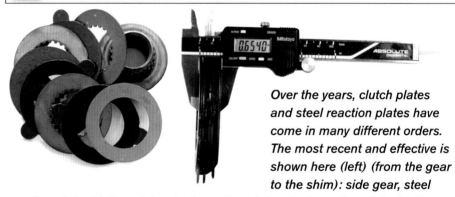

Over the years, clutch plates and steel reaction plates have come in many different orders. The most recent and effective is shown here (left) (from the gear to the shim): side gear, steel reaction plate, friction plate, steel reaction plate, steel reaction plate, friction plate, steel reaction plate, friction plate, and shim. So this clutch pack includes four steel plates, three friction plates, and one .020-inch-thick shim.

Notice that the steel reaction plates are splined on the inside diameter to align with the side gear; the friction plates are tabbed to align with the pockets in the differential case. Ideally you want the entire clutch pack, including the shim, to be about .640 to .645 inch for a stock clutch pack and as thick as .655 inch for a performance pack (right). In my opinion the thicker pack performs better and a few pops during turns from the clutch pack are acceptable because you know what is causing the pops and are not worried. Be sure you understand the pops if you are going to use the thicker pack values.

Here are all of the internal parts and gears of the limited-slip differential assembled just for visual reference. Keep in mind, you cannot install them in the differential case like this, but when the assembly has been rebuilt, all of these parts are arranged as shown. I leave the side gears and clutch packs pre-assembled as shown because they are ready to be installed in the differential case. Also the spherical pinion washers resting on the differential pin are important to include during the re-assembly process because they act as the wear surface between the hardened pinions and the differential case. They are curved to match the differential case and back surface of the pinions.

4 Inspect Differential Pocket

The differential pocket for the clutch plate alignment looks like this. The clutch plate tabs align with and run against this semi-circular pocket.

5 Install Side Gears and Clutch Packs

Install the completely assembled side gear with clutch pack into the differential case. Because there is no pre-load on pinion gears in the differential case, this is easy. The factory-painted orange side gears distinguish themselves from other gears.

Install the opposite-side gear with its clutch pack and shim in place. At this stage, nothing is holding the side gears in place, so they may fall out. Some people install long bolts with washers to help temporarily hold the gears in place. I typically use a 1/2-inch bolt with large washers that span the 6-inch-long holes. Since this is just an assembly aid, the nut just needs to be hand tight. A second set of hands helps, but I have been able to do it by myself; it just takes more time and patience.

6 Install Pinions

Install the differential pinions with their spherical thrust washers in the differential case. Since the gears are just being partially engaged you can assemble them by hand. Do not forget to include the thrust washers that go between the differential case and the pinion gears. Install both pinions at the same time and rotate the side gear to get the pinions to roll in place. (The home-made tool that was shown on page 39 is used to rotate the side gear. It is just a piece of an old axle shaft with a square plate welded to it.) Notice that this pinion gear thrust washer is in place between the pinion and the differential case.

Professional Mechanic Tip PRO TIP

7 Install Differential Pin

PRO TIP *The pinion gears must be aligned correctly, so the differential pin can slide right into place. Use a punch to push it through the pinion gear and into the correct position. Keep in mind, it is possible to assemble the differential gears one tooth off. If installed one tooth off, the differential pin does not line up correctly (left). You want the pinions to be 180 degrees apart and aligned to the correct side gear. So take the time now to make certain that the pin goes easily in place (right). It will be obvious if you are a tooth off. If so, just remove the pinions and index by one tooth with the side gear.*

8 Install Preload Spring

Once the differential gears align correctly, remove the differential pin and install one of the two S-shaped preload springs that came with your kit. For reference, the Ford car spring (PN E0AZ-4214-A) has a free height of approximately 1.510 inches and a Ford Racing truck or heavy-duty version (PN F3TZ-4214-A) is approximately 1.765 inches. The car unit was used from 1985 to 2000 while the truck version was originally used in the 1999 Cobra and all 2000-and-up V-8 Mustangs. (I always use a heavy-duty spring for any high-performance build because they are about the same price at about $2.)

Keep in mind that the downside to a tightly assembled and heavily preloaded limited-slip differential is additional wind-up and potential chatter and pops as the plates transition from sticking to slipping. Wear safety glasses. The spring needs to evenly descend into the assembly and between the side and pinion gears. If the spring doesn't start correctly, it may jump out.

You may want to place a shop rag over the spring to help keep it contained as you tap the spring into place with a hammer. You can also use channel-lock-style pliers or a C-clamp to pre-compress the spring. I have found that these aids just get in the way and make assembly more difficult. But some mechanics swear by the method of pre-collapsing the spring in a bench vise and holding it in this state with needle-nose Vise-Grips through a portion of the S-shape and then setting it partially in place prior to final placement with a soft-face hammer or brass punch.

9 Double-Check S-Spring is Centered

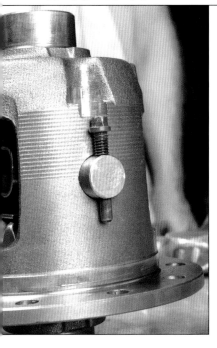

Once the spring has been installed, visually check that it is centered. Trial fit the differential pin again. Make sure the through hole in the differential pin is aligned with the hole in the differential case for the retention bolt. If it is not, use the retention bolt to rotate the pin to the correct orientation. This ensures that everything is aligned.

10 Push Pin in Place

When correct alignment of the S-spring has been verified, remove the retention bolt and push the pin in the remaining amount. Be careful not to push the pin in too far; it needs to be centered in the differential case so that the through hole aligns with the retention bolt (shown).

Temporarily install the retention bolt. Hand tighten the bolt by just a couple of threads to hold the pin in place.

The Traction-Lok limited-slip differential assembly is now completely assembled. You can set this aside now and concentrate on the axle housing.

Axle Housing, Wheel End Bearing and Seal Assembly

At this stage, the internal differential has been assembled, so focus your attention on the axle housing. You should assemble the wheel end bearings and seals and pre-assemble as many parts as possible before the ring-and-pinion gears go in place.

1 Verify Condition of Bearing and Seal Bores

Make sure that the bearing and seal bores are clean and free from any burrs before you start the assembly process. This is a perfectly clean wheel end assembly. The chances of your axle coming this clean is relatively low, but do the best you can to make sure that the seal bore is burr free.

2 Install Bearings

Install the axle shaft wheel end bearing, which is a cylindrical roller bearing with caged rollers. Use an old bearing race or any adequate diameter steel tube and a hammer to drive the bearing in place. Evenly apply force so the bearing is driven straight into the bore and seats in the bore. Be sure to drive the bearing to the bottom of the bore. (You hear a solid thud when the bearing is completely seated.) Pour some oil on the rollers and spread it around with your fingers so they are not dry on initial break-in of the axle.

3 Install Seals

Professional Mechanic Tip

Special Tool

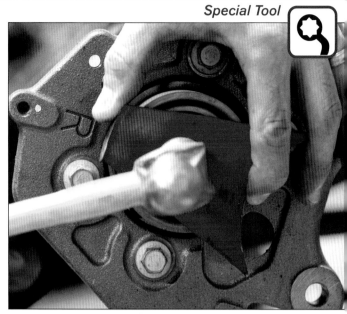

PRO TIP *Do not re-use any old axle shaft seals. This is a recipe for a leaking axle later. You can add a tiny bead of black RTV to the outside diameter of the seal as added insurance against leaking. This additional RTV helps prevent leaking, which may have been caused by rust during service. Evenly apply it by hand. You can also apply a small amount of grease on the seal lip by hand to help the axle shaft slide into place later.*

Use the correct diameter seal driver or a large enough socket to get the seal seated. If you do not have access to either, any steel plate that spans the seal diameter works. (Here, I am using my homemade shim driver tool to seat the seal.) Just make certain that the seal goes in straight and is fully seated. Repeat this procedure for the other side of the axle.

8.8-Inch Axle Bearing and Seal Update

In 2005 Ford changed the axle bearing and seal arrangement to a bearing outside diameter of 2.531 inches and an inside diameter of 1.619 inches. This is the M-1225-B1 bearing and seal kit.

Prior to that, 1986–2004, the part number is M-1225-B and the bearing outside diameter is 2.256 inches.

So make sure that you get the correct wheel end bearings and seals. ■

Ring and Pinion Gear Set Assembly

There are 33 different aftermarket shim thicknesses available, ranging from .307 to .241 inch (in .002-inch increments). One of the biggest frustrations in building these axles is that the thin shims in an aftermarket pack are very difficult to install without damaging them. And if you use the OEM shims you have a bunch of different sizes laying around. If you build a lot of differentials, it makes sense to have a variety of OEM shim thicknesses in your shop; otherwise, take your time with the aftermarket ones. This is also a reason to save any old shims for your next build.

The Ford base part number is 4067; you can purchase the exact thickness that you need from there. The Ford shims are pricey and that is why most people use an aftermarket shim pack, which consist of a "sandwich" of three shims. The inner and outer shims are thick, while the middle shim is thinner. The pack can be driven in with a brass drift without any concern for cracking. A final check of pattern and backlash is a good idea.

You can see how the parts fit in order. The pinion has a gear or head on one side and the spline and threads on the other.

The head shim and then the head bearing are pressed in place on the pinion. (This shim is what sets the pinion head mounting depth. If you do not have the original shim as a baseline, a .030-inch-thick shim is a good starting point for the 8.8-inch axles. If you are using another Ford gear set, all are really close and the original shim is a great starting point. I prefer the Ford gears as they are readily available, more consistent, and higher quality compared to aftermarket gears. If Ford does not produce the needed ratio you have to use aftermarket gears.)

Next come the pinion head and tail bearing cups that are pressed into the axle housing.

The collapsible spacer goes in between the head and the tail bearing cones. The head bearing cone is a press fit on the pinion shaft but the tail bearing cone is a slip fit. The collapsible spacer provides resistance to the tail bearing cone and allows for manufacturing differences in the housings.

There are solid shim kits available in the aftermarket. If you go this route, always add a shim .012 inch thicker than the original collapsible spacer height and continue decreasing the shim thickness until you achieve the correct torque-to-turn measurement. This makes certain that you do not overload and damage the bearings by not having a thick enough shim in place.

Next is the pinion seal oil slinger and seal that are pressed into the housing; and finally the input flange and nut.

1 Install Head and Tail Bearing Cups

These are the pinion head shims that come in a typical rebuild kit. The total shim range is .010 to .038 inch. These shims can be stacked to achieve the correct height. These shims are used to compensate for variations in production tolerances, specifically the variation of the housing machining and gears. As mentioned earlier, Ford gears are very consistent and the main source of variation is from the housing machining.

Again, make sure the housing is clean, and rinse out any debris from the oil feed and return ports. From the backside of the axle, drive in the pinion head bearing outer race, or cup. Make sure that it is fully seated and exercise extreme care to not hit the tapered race. Drive on the thin outer diameter of the bearing cup. If you have an old cup or the correct size bearing driver, use one of them. These are strongly recommended for driving the new cup, but you can also get away with a punch, but exercise care not to hit the tapered surface. Make sure that the cup is seated squarely into the axle housing.

Follow the same procedure to install the tail bearing cup in the front of the axle. Set in the tail bearing cup and drive in the pinion seal. The pinion seal actually traps the tail bearing in place, so don't install the pinion seal without the bearing in place.

2 Set Pinion Bearing at Correct Depth

Here the pinion head shim is in place. The head bearing is propped up to show the shim. Press fit this bearing onto the pinion shaft. If the shim is incorrect, you must remove the bearing in order to remove the shim. When you remove the bearing, make sure that you grab the bearing inner race and not the cage to make the shim adjustment. A bearing spreader (such as the one shown in Step 13 on page 37) is required to properly grab the bearing race. If you grab the cage and remove the bearing, you will distort the cage and ruin the bearing. Make or purchase a set-up bearing so you avoid bearing damage when you remove it from the pinion shaft. If you perform a number of axle rebuilds, this tool comes in very handy. You can get a bearing with the inside diameter opened up to allow for a slip fit (for about $70) or you can simply take a die grinder to the inside diameter of a new bearing to make it larger.

When you have determined the correct shim thickness, use the correct press-fit bearing and a new collapsible spacer to replace the set-up bearing. While this may sound like a hassle, you need to do this correctly because you need to achieve the correct gear position for the best differential performance and reliability.

3 Shim Pinion Head

Some tools make shimming the pinion head easier, but they only work if the new pinion head is marked with its deviation from the ideal condition. Some aftermarket gears are marked, but the Ford Motorsports gears and original equipment gears are not marked. The tool (left) comes with good instructions if you are fortunate enough to have the pinion head markings. I actually own this tool and as you can tell by the lack of wear on it, I never use it. A typical aftermarket gear set (right) has the mounting distance offset and backlash values engraved on it.

4 Press Shim and Head Bearing into Place

Press the pinion head bearing and shim into place (left). You can use an old bearing race as a press tool because you are sure to only press on the bearing race and not the bearing cage. Tapered bearings are very sensitive to roller positioning and it is crucial that you never press on the cage. Any damage to the cage misaligns the rollers and the bearings fail. On the right are some scrap pieces of various diameters are useful for pressing bearings and seals in place.

5 Install Pinion in Axle Housing

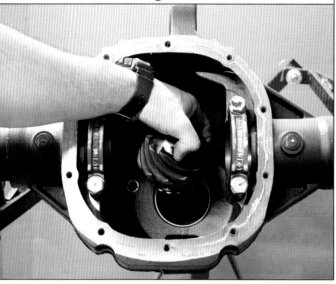

Always lubricate the bearings with fresh gear oil prior to assembly in the housing. Place the collapsible spacer on the pinion and put the pinion in place. Add some gear lube to the bearings and spin the pinion to check for smooth running. Install from the back side of the housing.

6 Inspect Pinion Installation

This is what the front side of the axle housing looks like. You can see that the seal is in place along with the tail bearing behind it and the pinion stem is partially sticking out. Be careful, especially when working with the axle still in the vehicle that the pinion does not fall out. There is really nothing holding it in place until the flange is installed.

7 Set Flange in Correct Position

Position the flange in place. I recommend applying grease to the seal and putting a small amount of grease on the seal surface of the flange. This flange also has a brown plastic dust excluder installed to shield the seal from road debris.

8 Install Pinion Nut

Install the flange nut and start the process of achieving the correct bearing preload. Always use a new pinion nut on the final installation because it has fresh Loctite on the threads and sealant on the flanged surface. During the bearing preload process, make sure that you rotate the bearing frequently to ensure proper torque-to-turn readings. Also, never back off the pinion nut to reduce preload. If the preload is too high, you need to replace the collapsible spacer and start over. I usually purchase extra collapsible spacers just in case this happens.

9 Install Flange

A few different styles of tool can be used to hold the flange in place while you are tightening the pinion nut. A Ratech tool (bottom) can be purchased inexpensively or a simple homemade tool (top) can be fabricated. Keep in mind that achieving a torque of 250 ft-lbs is not unheard of in order to get the collapsible spacer to begin yielding. A long-handled tool on the breaker bar are usually required to hold the flange in place.

Check the pattern to be sure there is no need to set the preload; rather, you just need to take up any clearance in the bearings.

If you need to set the preload, be careful not to over tighten. You want the torque-to-turn to be between 16 and 28 in-lbs for new bearings and 8 to 14 in-lbs for used bearings (see page 94 for details on the torque-to-turn measuring process).

You can assemble the axle on a stand (shown) or in the car. If you assemble the axle while it is installed in the car, it is important to either have a hoist or get the car as high as possible on jack stands, so you have room to swing the long-handled tools while the collapsible spacer is installed.

This homemade flange tool is used for U-joint–style flanges. The tool does not have to be fancy, just attached firmly and long enough for adequate leverage.

10 Clean Ring Gear

Make certain that there are no burrs on the mounting surface of the ring gear. Run a fine file across the face just to make sure. Use solvent to clean the ring gear thread holes and the entire gear. The entire gear as well as the holes need to be clean of any oil and debris or any metal shavings prior to installation on the differential case.

Torque Fasteners

11 Install Ring Gear in Case

The ring gear is a clearance fit over the differential, except for the last 1/2 inch, which is the press-fit pilot diameter. One method to install the ring gear in the differential case begins with setting the ring gear in place and starting all of the ring gear bolts. I always re-use either the factory bolts with fresh Loctite or get new fasteners from Ford directly. If you are going to re-use the factory bolts, make sure they are clean before applying fresh Loctite. You do not want any traces of oil that makes the Loctite fail later. Tighten the bolts in stages in a crisscross pattern to achieve the final torque of 100 ft-lbs recommended for Ford Motorsports gears. I do this in five steps: snug the bolts down by hand, then torque to 25, 50, 75, and then 100 ft-lbs. Start with a low torque to evenly pull the gear in place. You never want to excessively load the bolt threads when they are partially engaged because you may strip the threads.

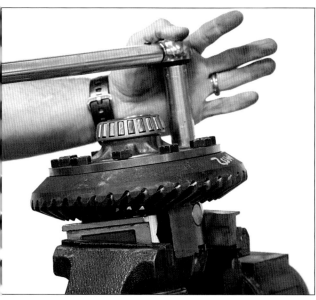

Another method to install the ring gear on the differential case begins with putting the differential case in a bench vise with soft jaws to avoid knicking the differential case. You install the bolts to act as guide pins and then use a press to force the ring gear in place. I am not in favor of this method because you risk chipping or cracking the gear teeth, but with care and a soft surface such as blocks of wood to press against, it is acceptable.

12 Compare Factory and Aftermarket Ring Bolts

Here is a comparison of the factory ring gear bolts (left) and the typical aftermarket bolts (right) that are supplied in most rebuild kits. The aftermarket bolts always seem of marginal quality to me, with the exception of a premium aftermarket brand such as ARP. I always choose to re-use the factory bolts over using the aftermarket ones. Of course, the ideal situation is to get new bolts, as most of the new applications use torque-to-yield fasteners that really should not be re-used.

13 Press On Differential Case Bearings

Similar to pinion head bearings, differential case bearings are a press fit. Use an old bearing race as a press tool and press just on the inner race. No shims go underneath these bearings. Just make sure that the bearings are fully seated. Shims that go between the bearing cup and the axle housing establish the ring gear position and bearing preload.

Re-use the original shims and check backlash and pattern (see Chapter 7). Just as with the pinion shim, some adjustments may be required. Install the old left-hand (ring gear) side shim and then use a thinner shim on the right side to make it easier to install the differential for this first fit up. No play side-to-side can be present in the differential. You can take care of bearing preload shimming at the final installation, once you have the gear pattern and backlash setting correct.

14 Mate Axle to Differential

Here, the differential shim is partially in place. It is the cast-iron steel ring with the light green and black stripes on it. The beveled edge goes toward the outside of the axle. It is an interference fit to re-install the differential. Be careful; the differential is heavy and awkward to install, and you don't want to drop it. Partially install the differential with the bearing cups and angle the shims in place. Note the two punch marks above the bearing cap surface inside the axle housing. These are the marks for the bearings caps.

15 Select Shim Driver Tool

Since the shim is press fit, use the shim driver tool to install it. Do not hit the cast-iron shims directly with a hammer because they are very brittle and will crack. You can purchase aftermarket steel "super shim" packs that are not cast.

You can use a mill or a belt sander to make your own tool like the one (left) I cut out of flat plate. Be sure the curved shape accurately matches the shim diameter.

You can also purchase a tool (right) that is actually a series of different curved shapes to fit just about any axle. Yukon Tool makes versions of both of these.

16 Install Bearing Caps and Bolts

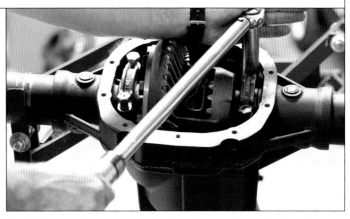

Once the shims and bearing cups are driven in place (left), install the bearing caps and bolts. Remember, during the disassembly process, the caps were marked so they are oriented correctly from left to right and top to bottom. Ensure they go back into the original place and orientation. The bolt torque is 90 to 100 ft-lbs; tighten them in stages, just like ring gear bolts (right). I always use 90 ft-lbs to be safe.

17 Check Backlash and Pattern

Set up a dial indicator and verify backlash and pattern one last time. The dial indicator base has a magnetic portion that is temporarily attached to the axle housing; the dial position is adjusted to get the dial pointer in the correct position. Once in place, the dial face can be rotated to align with the zero position of the gauge. Check backlash in at least four different positions that are about 90 degrees apart from one another; there should not be more than .004-inch variation. The backlash should be .008 to .012 inch.

New gear sets come with a backlash recommendation in the instructions. Always use the backlash that the gear manufacturer recommends. If the backlash is not within specification, change the shim thicknesses accordingly to achieve the correct backlash.

To increase backlash, move the ring gear farther to the left by decreasing that shim's thickness. The amount of decrease on the left shim is the same amount that you need to add to the right shim in order to maintain the overall bearing width and zero endplay.

Once the backlash is correct and you are satisfied with the pattern (see Chapter 7), then you need to achieve the correct bearing preload on these bearings. If you are using aftermarket shims, add .006-inch shim thickness per side. The aftermarket units are thin shims stacked behind the factory cast-iron shims. Install the thin shims first and then drive in the thicker shim. The other option is to have an assortment of OEM-style cast-iron shims on hand.

Change in Backlash (inch)	Change in Shim Thickness (inch)	Change in Backlash (inch)	Change in Shim Thickness (inch)
.001	.002	.009	.012
.002	.002	.010	.014
.003	.004	.011	.014
.004	.006	.012	.016
.005	.006	.013	.018
.006	.008	.014	.018
.007	.010	.015	.020
.008	.010		

This chart shows the required change in shim thickness as compared to backlash change. It is not always a one-to-one relationship.

18 Install Axle Shafts

First, remove the differential pin retention cross bolt that was partially installed earlier and then remove the differential pin. Remove the pin to allow the axle shaft to go in farther than typical (see Chapter 3). This gives access to the C-washer groove. A small O-ring was installed in the groove of the stock axle shafts to help hold the C-washer in place during the initial build at the axle assembly plant. These O-rings are usually long gone by the time the axles are repaired, so don't worry if they are missing because they are not critical.

As during the disassembly process, always guide the axle shaft carefully through the axle seal. If the spline is dragged across the seal, seal damage will result. If the weight of the shaft drags across the seal, the garter spring can be knocked off the seal. The last couple of inches are a little tricky because the splines need to be aligned. Just lightly tip the flange up and down and the shaft eventually lines up.

19 Install C-Washers

Torque Fasteners

Carefully reach in behind the S-spring and install the C-washer. Use a small screwdriver to fully seat it and make certain that it is all the way in place. For clarity, this photo shows the installation outside the axle and without the ring gear. (This is actually done after the ring gear is installed and the differential is in the axle housing.)

When the washer has been fully seated in the axle shaft groove, pull the axle outboard; the washer becomes trapped in the pocket that is machined in the side gear. Although not readily apparent, the gold colored washer is nested in the pocket. Repeat this procedure for the other side and then install the differential pin. Torque the retention bolt to 26 ft-lbs.

I like to use a new retention bolt and most rebuild kits come with one, so be sure to use it. The new ones already have Loctite on the threads but if you re-use the old bolt, make sure that it is clean and dry and add Loctite to the threads. You never want any of the bolts to come loose inside the axle housing.

20 Install Axle Cover on Housing

You can use RTV sealant to seal the axle cover on the housing. Use a bead of black RTV sealant and let the sealant cure, overnight if possible, prior to filling the axle with oil. RTV is a condensation cure product, but if there is too much humidity (70 to 80 percent), it actually slows the curing process. So you need to work fast! Apply the RTV and get the cover bolted down within 5 minutes to be on the safe side.

Using a paper-style gasket is another way to seal the axle cover on the housing. Apply a thin layer of gasket adhesive on both sides. The sealant needs some cure time before it is exposed to the gear oil. I recommend waiting at least 60 minutes before you add oil; overnight is better.

Torque Fasteners

21 Install Axle Cover Bolts

Use a crisscross pattern to tighten the bolts. First snug up the bolts, then torque them to 33 ft-lbs for steel covers and 24 ft-lbs for aluminum covers.

22 Fill Differential with Fluid

If you have a limited-slip differential, add 4 ounces of correct friction modifier. Typically for the 8.8-inch axle, the fill amount is about 2½ quarts to the bottom of the fill hole when the vehicle is level. This photo shows the fill hole with the 3/8-inch square drive plug. This plug and housing are brand new; most are rusty and the square drive recess is full of debris. Make sure that you take the time to clean it out and fully seat the drive tool or you will strip the plug. (There is a picture of this in in Step 1 on page 61). The fill plug is on the driver's side on the forward-facing, vertical surface next to the pinion.

TECH TIP — Pinion Head Bearing

In 2010, Ford started using a different pinion head bearing in Mustang GT and GT500 axles. This new bearing is correct for all of the newer axles and can be used in the 1986–2009 housing.

Also, not all axles used the oil slinger but most modern units have it. Its main purpose is to limit the amount of oil to the seal and avoid flooding the seal with oil. ■

TECH TIP — Torque Values

Some aftermarket gears require a lower ring gear torque value. Make sure to check the torque recommendations if you are not using an original Ford gear set. I have seen recommendations as low as 60 ft-lbs. Using the Ford Motorsports gears for any 8.8-inch build is recommended. ■

9-INCH DISASSEMBLY AND INSPECTION

Before I delve into the details of disassembling a 9-inch, let's review some basic information about the different years of production.

Physical Differences

The 1957 model-year axles have no dimples on the back round section, there is a flat band that runs vertically up the center of the rear cover, and there is a drain plug on the bottom of the housing.

The 1958 and 1959 models have two dimples on the back of housing, the same center vertical band as the 1957 unit, and not all have drain plugs. The 1960–1967 model years have the two dimples and the vertical center band but now have an oil-level plug in the back cover.

From about 1961 to 1972 the 9⅜-inch axles came on the scene.

Strength Differences

Some axles are inherently stronger than others. The 1967–1973 Cougar and Mustang units are the lightest duty with the thinnest wall

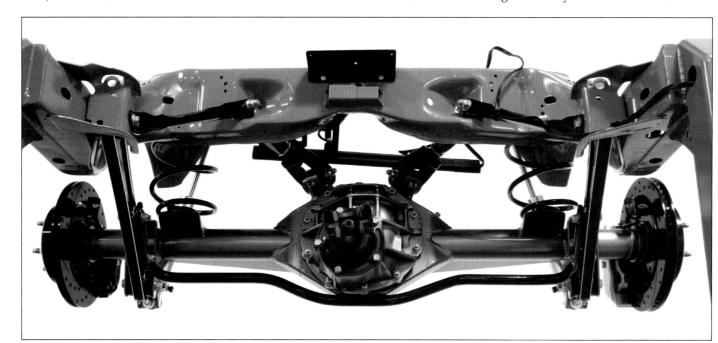

Here is a crate 9-inch axle for the GM A-Body/Chevelle. This is an excellent performance upgrade and available basically off the shelf. It even can be set up with disc brakes, a nodular third member, and be ready to drop right in your car.

Differential Component ID

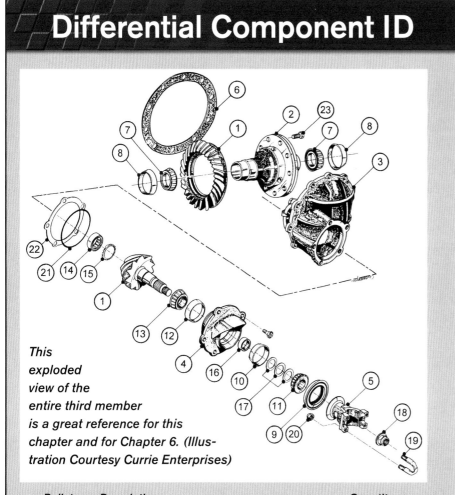

This exploded view of the entire third member is a great reference for this chapter and for Chapter 6. (Illustration Courtesy Currie Enterprises)

Bullet Number	Description	Quantity
1	Ring and pinion gear set	1
2	Differential assembly	1
3	Gear case (unassembled)	1
4	Pinion cartridge	1
5	Pinion flange (or yoke)	1
6	Gear case gasket	1
7	Differential bearing cone	2
8	Differential bearing cup	2
9	Pinion seal	1
10	Pinion tail bearing cup	1
11	Pinion tail bearing cone	1
12	Pinion head bearing cup	1
13	Pinion head bearing cone	1
14	Pinion pilot bearing	1
15	Pinion pilot bearing retainer	1
16	Pinion bearing preload solid spacer	1
17	Pinion bearing preload solid spacer shims	As required
18	Pinion nut	1
19	U-joint strap	2
20	U-joint strap nut	4
21	Pinion cartridge/O-ring	1
22	Pinion mounting distance shim	1
23	Ring gear bolt	10
—	Pinion cartridge bolt (not labeled)	5

housing material. They also have the smallest axle bearings.

The 1957–1969 heavy passenger car and truck axles (excluding Bronco) are stronger than the Cougar/Mustang units. These units also have the 3.25-inch-diameter axle tubes with flat tops.

The 1969–1977 housings are also desirable as they have the same larger-diameter tubes, and this larger diameter continues all the way to the wheel end bearing flange. The typical wall thickness for the factory housing is .177 inch while many of the aftermarket units have a thicker wall, .200 inch.

So, even though there may be some cheap axles available in the scrap yards, be careful as these are weaker and may require extensive repair just based on the abuse they have seen over the years. The aftermarket units use better, thicker, and stronger materials than the OEM units. In the long run, it is often less expensive to get a fresh housing than try to refurbish an old worn-out unit. Plus, when the old unit is finally repaired, it is still inferior to the new aftermarket units.

Axle Shaft Splines

For any performance build a 31-tooth spline (or more) is a must. The visual telltale sign of a 31-tooth spline axle shaft is the two counter-bored holes that are inline with the counter-sunk center on the end face of the axle shaft hub. Some have an Oval-shaped recess like the 28-tooth axles.

The 28-tooth spline axles shafts have an oval-shaped recess on the end of the axle shaft hub. Some have an oval-shaped recess like the 28-tooth axles.

See page 18 for a photo showing the difference between a 28- and a 31-tooth spline.

Disassembly Procedure

In order to assess the amount of repair required, you first need to disassemble part of or all of your axle assembly. This is followed by careful inspection and, at times, measurement of the parts. There are certain items that should be replaced with any disassembly and re-assembly process, such as seals, bearings, O-rings, and oil.

Because there are so many variants of these axles, there may be some slight differences to your specific application.

Brake Drum and Axle Shaft Disassembly

The first step is to have the vehicle on jack stands and the wheels and tires removed. After you remove the brake drums be sure to set them aside in a clean and safe place. Remember to label the axle shafts according to the side in which they were installed, as they are different lengths. There is an access hole in the wheel flange that allows you to get a socket on the nut that holds the axle shaft and brake backing plate in place. The rest, as they say, is a piece of cake.

The access hole is in the wheel-mounting flange portion of the axle shaft and between two of the lug studs. Here you can see one of the nuts that retains the axle shaft. Four of these fasteners need to be removed so the axle shaft can be removed.

1 Loosen Nuts

Use the correct-size deep-well socket or a shallow socket with an extension to reach in and loosen the four lock nuts nuts (a deep-well socket avoids the socket falling off the extension and having to fish the socket out from behind the axle flange). Notice that the brake hardware is in place.

2 Remove Nuts

Once the nuts are loose, reach behind the flange to retrieve them. (This backing plate has the brake shoes and hardware already removed.) You can leave the brake hardware in place or remove it. Keep in mind that removing the brake hardware prior to the axle shafts makes the job a little easier.

Your overall plan is also a factor. If you have fresh brakes and are going to retain the drum style, then it makes sense to leave the brakes attached to the backing plates. If you want to remove all the rust and repaint the backing plates, the brake hardware needs to be removed.

3 Loosen Axle Shaft Plate

The rectangular shaped steel plate under the nuts holds the axle shafts and bearings in the housing. Once the nuts have been removed, you can lightly pull the plate loose. It is still trapped on the axle shaft, but you need to make sure it is loose. Be careful because it may move around a little.

Special Tool

4 Remove Axle Shaft

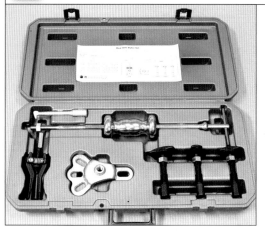

Use a slide hammer tool, such as this one, to pop the axle shaft loose. It's a great tool to have in your shop, but runs about $150. You can use pry bars to dislodge the axle shaft but be careful not to bend the plates. (Later, you'll see how the bearing arrangement traps the plates on the axle shafts.) If you are going to re-use the bearings, the plates are also re-used. I strongly recommend replacing the bearings at the same time because it's a minimal investment to ensure good performance.

Attach the slide hammer tool to the axle shaft wheel hub. The base of the puller slips over the wheel's studs and the bolts secure the puller to the hub. A couple of quick pulls and the shaft should be loose. This tool really makes this job simple and effortless.

Partially remove the axle shaft. Notice how the ball bearing traps the retainer plate on the axle shaft. The retainer ring is to the left of the ball bearing. This ring keeps the axle bearing on the axle shaft. Also notice the polished section to the left of the ring from the seal riding on the journal. This is a common sealed ball bearing wheel end arrangement.

Once the axle shaft has been completely removed, inspect the bearing and seal surface. I recommend replacing the bearings for any rebuild, but if they are in good condition, you may get away with re-using them. But it's a risk.

This axle shaft uses the large ball bearing arrangement. This sealed-style bearing cannot be re-greased. You can see the wear mark from the seal. If yours has a groove, replace the shaft. If it is a big-bearing shaft, you may want to upgrade to the stronger, tapered-bearing arrangement. The housing accommodates the larger tapered bearing; it just requires a different axle shaft.

A production axle shaft end never touches the differential pin, in contrast to to the semi-float style used on Ford 8.8-inch axles. For this reason, this very rough cut end was common from Ford during high-volume production. Aftermarket shafts are never this roughly cut.

5 Remove Brake Backing Plates

Remove the brake backing plates for cleaning and painting. (The brake lines should have already been removed from the wheel cylinders.) Lightly tap around the backing plates to remove them. They usually come off with little effort.

6 Seal Inside of Housing

Once the axle shaft has been removed, look for the seal inside of the housing. This seal keeps the gear oil in the axle for ball-bearing wheel ends. The tapered-bearing style of wheel ends do not use this seal as they share oil with the axle. Note that this axle flange shows signs of the original gasket and sealant. This needs to be cleaned off and prepped before re-assembly. The T-bolts can be pushed out now.

7 Remove Retainer Ring

Replacing the bearings and retainer plates means that you need to remove the retainer ring from the axle shaft. One method is to partially drill through the ring and then press the bearing off. The ring has a significant press fit, so it's very difficult to press off. Remember, this is holding the wheel on the vehicle and you might have to destroy it. A quick center punch on the ring in the middle of the unit acts as a guide for the drill.

Using a 1/4-inch bit drill partially into the ring making certain to center the hole. Being very careful, set the drill on a low-RPM setting and drill almost to the bottom. To avoid drilling too deep you can mark the desired depth on the bit with tape, but still stop and check often. If you drill too deep, you'll actually drill into the axle shaft. If this happens, you need to replace the axle shaft because it creates a stress riser in a critical area, and the axle will probably break in this area.

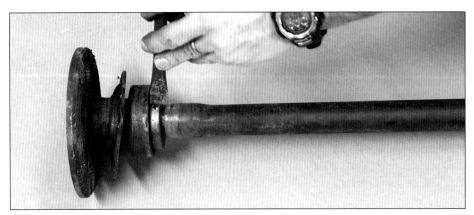

Using a hammer and chisel, solidly strike the ring at the drilled section. If you support the other side of the ring with a block of wood you can hammer away.

Here you can see the slight crack in the retaining ring. This is all that is required to relieve the press fit. Now you can use a typical bearing puller tool and shop press to remove the retainer, bearing, and plate.

Third Member and Pinion Cartridge Removal

Now that you have the wheel ends and axle shafts sorted out, you can concentrate on the third member and pinion cartridge. You can remove the pinion cartridge from the third member while the third member is still in place on the housing, but the order does not matter, especially if you know that you are going to upgrade the pinion cartridge to the larger Daytona-style bearing support.

As a matter of fact, more often than not, there is no reason to re-use the stock third member for any performance-style vehicle when so many stronger nodular units are available in the aftermarket. Chances are that you will be replacing everything unless you are doing a stock rebuild.

1 Remove Fill Plug

Before proceeding, remove the fill plug. This particular example is full of dirt and crud. Use a small flathead screwdriver or pick to clean it out, so that a 3/8-inch square drive fits properly.

Here, the 3/8-inch drive was not tapped all the way in place. Most 3/8-inch extensions have a spring-loaded ball that helps hold the socket in place. Be sure that you tap in and fully seat the extension. If not, the plug starts to strip out as shown here.

2 Remove Pinion Cartridge

Five bolts hold the pinion cartridge in place. Use a ratchet and socket or wrench to remove them. The pinion cartridge supports the pinion bearings and the pinion itself, plus a shim also resides between the cartridge and the housing. This shim sets the pinion mounting depth. Typical shim sizes range from .008 to .021 inch with the nominal thickness being .015.

Use a hammer and punch to tap on the pinion in a few different spots to help free it. Keep in mind that the cartridge is held very tightly in the housing and needs to come out straight. Be careful to not tilt the unit. Also be careful not to pry on the cartridge too aggressively. Countless tabs have been cracked off, turning these cartridges into scrap. Another option is to attach a slide hammer to the pinion yoke to remove the cartridge.

Precision Measurement, Documentation Required

2 Remove Pinion Cartridge *CONTINUED*

  The O-ring is still in place on the pinion cartridge. The pinion depth shim is hanging near the pinion. Keep track of this shim if you are going to re-use the gear set. Even if you go with a new gear set, you should determine the thickness of this old shim for reference. The difference from nominal is marked on some gears on the pinion head, so the correct shim thickness can be easily determined. This marking isn't always present, so you may need to do some research in service manuals or literature from new-gear providers.

3 Inspect Pinion Trunnion

Once the pinion has been removed, you have your first look at the ring gear and the internals of the gear case. Inspect the pinion straddle support and retainer. Clean the pinion trunnion of any gear oil and debris. The trunnion should be round and smooth without any signs of grooves or gouges. This unit still has the bearing and retainer in place and they look okay. Examine the pinion trunnion for any signs of wear. Besides having sludgy appearing oil, this unit is in good condition. The oil appears to have been contaminated with water and is thicker (like pudding) and has a grayish color.

This is a worn pinion trunnion. This pinion needs to be scrapped. Since the hypoid gears are a matched set, both ring and pinion gears need to be replaced. You can use a speedi-sleeve to try to salvage a gear set. However, if the gear set has enough wear to damage this area of the pinion, it necessitates replacing the gear set.

4 Inspect Pinion Straddle-Mounted Bearing Support

Severe overloading has cracked this pinion straddle-mounted bearing support. This unit also had enough deflection from excessive torque so that the gear teeth climbed over one another and pushed the differential case through the bearing caps. This is a testament to why you want to use a nodular third member for any high-performance applications.

5 Disassemble Pinion Cartridge

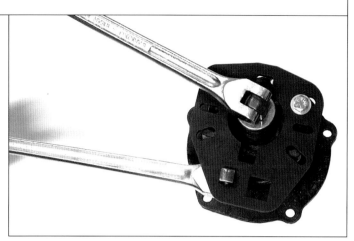

This is a typical pinion flange puller tool that can be purchased, but you can easily make one (see page 50). In order to loosen the pinion nut, you can use an impact gun or you can use a tool to hold the flange stationary while loosening the nut. The impact gun works fine, but needs a means to hold the flange later during re-assembly.

Bolting the flange-holding tool to the flange with two bolts stops it from rotating with a breaker bar. Use the correct-size socket along with another breaker bar to loosen the pinion nut. The pinion nut is very tight so you may need to use some torque to break it loose. Don't be shy; apply ample force to loosen the nut.

6 Pull Flange from Pinion

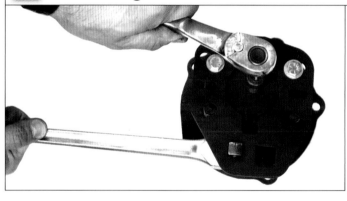

The flange-holder tool also acts as a flange puller. Typically the pinion flange spline has a slight helix built into it. This helix takes out any potential backlash in the spline and minimizes clunk. This helix also makes it difficult to remove and install the flange, so a puller is required to remove the flange. Use a two-jaw puller or even a harmonic balancer puller. Attach it to the flange and apply the appropriate force.

7 Index Pinion and Flange

Remove the nut then use a paint pen to mark the flange and the pinion where they come in contact. This properly indexes these parts for re-assembly. Or you can make light dimples with a center punch, which will not be removed when you clean the parts in solvent.

In some cases, the flanges are balanced as a complete axle assembly so you need to reassemble them in the correct alignment. Otherwise, the axle assembly is out of balance and can create excessive vibration in the vehicle. Obviously, if you are changing the ratio, you don't need to worry about this.

8 Remove Pinion from Cartridge

The pinion head bearing is still pressed on the pinion shaft. You can see the stock collapsible spacer sitting on the splines. The bearing races or cones are still pressed into the cartridge. Knock out the pinion seal to get the tail bearing out with a hammer and punch from the back side. When these parts have been pressed apart, the basic arrangement of the parts looks like this. Some units have an oil slinger between the tail bearing and the seal.

If you are replacing the bearings, use a hammer and punch to remove the races from the cartridge. Make sure that the cartridge is fully supported on the main round body portion of the casting and not the weaker mounting tabs, which can easily crack off.

9 Remove Gears from Third Member

The bearing caps are machined in place with the gear case. You will need to return them to their original position and orientation (as with the 8.8-inch axle and engine main bearing caps). To help with this, I recommend stamping them with numbers. (I have highlighted my numbers in yellow in this photo to help them stand out.) Or you can use dimples; one for one side and two for the other side. Then remove them.

Two different style bearing pullers are available on the market. Both work well. The clam-shell unit (above) is a special tool designed just for pinions. The fairly common bearing splitter style (top) is more versatile and economic.

10 Remove Keepers

Differential bearings are preloaded; large adjuster nuts set the ring gear mounting distance. The adjuster nuts have a positive anti-rotation feature: keepers that are bolted to the bearing cap. Remove the bolt.

10 Remove Keepers
CONTINUED

The keeper is U-shaped and fits into the hole in the adjuster nut. Move the keeper out of the adjuster nut hole by sliding out the keeper tab.

11 Remove Bearing Bolts and Caps

Use a standard socket and ratchet to loosen and remove the four bolts that secure the differential bearings in place. Notice that I stuck one of the axle shafts into the differential to help hold the third member from rotating. An impact gun also can be used to loosen these bolts.

Critical Inspection

12 Remove Adjuster Nut

Once the caps have been removed, loosen the adjuster nut. Usually, you can unthread it by hand. If the adjuster nut is stubbornly fastened and you don't want to invest in special tools, use a couple screw drivers in two of the holes to loosen it.

Closely inspect the inner surface of the adjuster nut where it meets the differential bearing cup. Often there is a slight wear groove in the adjuster. This can be erased with a few passes of a fine-tooth 1½-inch-wide flat file. You want to make certain that the surface is as flat as possible.

There are two available nuts for 9-inch axles. The 8-inch and small 9-inch nuts have the same outside diameter. The 2.891-inch nut is shown on the left while the 3.063-inch nut is shown on the right, which is standard for 31-spline axles and the 9⅜-inch. The 3.250-inch (not shown) is the typical aftermarket version for large spline counts. Both sizes have the same thread pitch and number of notches. This means that indexing the nut a single notch of rotational motion equals .005 inch of axial movement.

13 Remove Differential from Gear Case

Here the bearing caps and bolts, along with the adjuster nuts and differential bearing cups, have been removed. Now just grab the differential case and lift it out of the gear case.

14 Inspect Gear Case

Close inspection of the internal components and the case usually uncovers any sign of concern, such as cracks. If the internal components are worn excessively and the case is questionable, it may make sense to Magnaflux the case or just replace it with a new nodular unit for any performance application.

You can also remove and replace the pinion support pocket bearing. The bearing is held in place with a metal retainer. If you are careful and don't deform the metal ring, you can re-use it. See page 97 for a picture of the sheet metal bearing retainer.

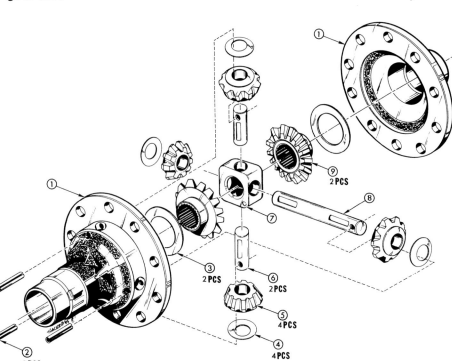

This exploded view of a traditional open differential shows the order of parts including flange (1), shim (3 and 4), and pinion gear (9). The open differential uses common side gears while the Traction-Lok differentials use two different side gears (5). This differential is similar to the unit that I will disassemble, but this one has four pinions instead of two (8). The additional pinions increase the torque-carrying capacity of this differential. This differential also has additional corresponding roll pins (6), a differential pin support block (7), and differential pins (2). (Illustration Courtesy Currie Enterprises)

This open differential carries two pinions. The pinion shaft is held in place with a single roll pin, which can be seen here at the 12 o'clock position, just below the ring gear inside diameter.

15 Drive Out Roll Pin

Use the appropriate-size punch to drive out the roll pin. You can use a long, 1/4-inch punch. You can remove the pin now or wait until the ring is removed. The order doesn't matter.

16 Remove Ring Gear

Remove the ring gear so you can remove the gear itself from the differential case. This is simply a matter of removing the ten bolts. These bolts are tight and require 80 ft-lbs or more of torque to remove. You can use an impact gun for this operation.

Place the differential on a block of wood or something soft to catch the gear. With a hammer, hit the punch to drive the ring gear through the bottom of the ring gear bolt holes. Make sure the punch is contacting the gear itself and not the threads on the side. Never hit the gear directly with a hammer. This will surely damage the gear and force replacement.

17 Separate Differential Case Halves

The differential case halves should come apart easily. Since this is an open differential, there are no other fasteners or clutch pack preload to overcome to separate them.

If your unit is difficult to separate, and this one was quite stubborn, you may need to resort to some persuasion with a hammer. Lightly tap the differential at the split line and alternate around the differential. Be careful as the casting differential is soft and you don't want to dent it. If there are any dents or dings, make sure to file them smooth before re-assembly.

Some mechanics mark the halves for clocking purposes, but the open differential only re-assembles in one way based on the orientation of the differential roll pin.

18 Inspect Case Internals

Once the case halves have been separated, you can see the internals. You can see the side gear on the left case half and the two pinions with the differential pin still in place on the right half. These pinions trap the other side's gear in place. Be sure to look for signs of wear and scoring on both halves.

19 Remove Differential Pin

Remove the differential pin so the pinions come out. This pin was stuck in position and required some persuasion with a hammer and punch. The pin should slide out with hand pressure. The fact that this pin was so difficult to remove indicates worn ridges.

20 Open Differential

All of the components removed from the open differential are shown here. They are arranged to show both sides of the pinions and side gears. Also note that there are hardened washers behind each side gear and pinion gear. These protect the softer cast-iron differential case from the gears wearing into them excessively.

21 Inspect Pinion Washers

This is the inside surface of one of the pinion washers. It is where the gear runs. Wear and debris contamination led to the washer's gouged wear surface. When this amount of wear is found, the washers should be replaced and I recommend replacing the entire differential. For a performance build, you want some type of limited-slip differential anyway.

22 Inspect Differential Pins

This differential pin shows signs of wear, and the pinion bores are just as worn. Under close examination, this pin actually has a step and gouges in the area where the pinions run. This kind of wear is commonly found when a differential has been installed in a vehicle that has been exposed to excessive tire spin. This excessive tire spin causes a high-speed difference between the pinion gear and this shaft, which definitely needs replacing.

Summary

You have completely disassembled the axle, removed the hypoid ring and pinion gears, and disassembled the differential. Now would be a good time to clean off the components that you are going to re-use, before you move on to re-assembly.

There are tons of replacement parts available for these axles. Many of the components are being reproduced to higher standards than the original components. If any of your components are suspect, it will be worthwhile in the long run to just get replacements.

You may also want to take the time to paint or powdercoat your housing. However, I strongly recommend against powdercoating the gear case or pinion support, as there will more often than not be powder in an area that you don't want it. If the powder gets inside the third member, it creates problems and is difficult to remove.

The exploded views of the torque-sensing limited-slip and the Traction-Lok will be valuable references while you are working on these differentials. The only difference between them is the addition of the preload springs on the Traction-Lok style.

Limited-slip differentials use four pinions. There are two versions. The top exploded view uses just side-gear separating forces to apply the clutch pack and is the Currie T.S.D. (torque-sensing differential). The bottom exploded view is the production-style factory limited-slip differential that uses additional springs to further apply the clutch pack. (Illustrations Courtesy Currie Enterprises)

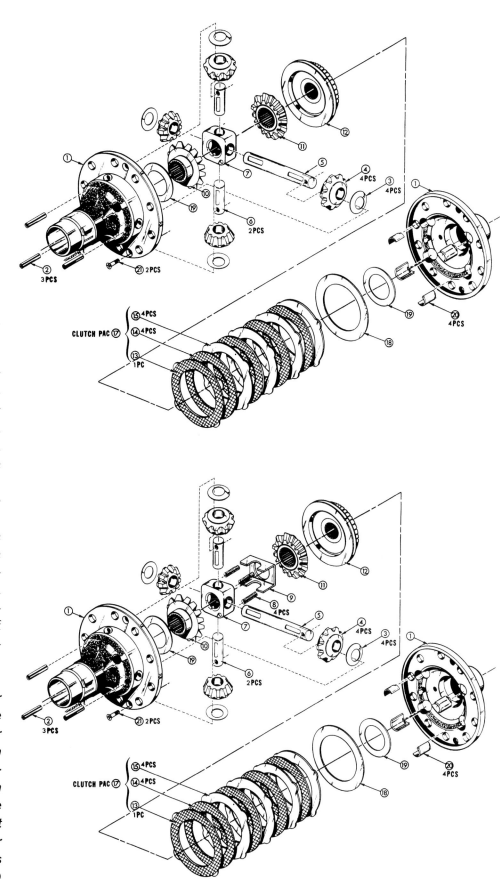

9-INCH AXLE ASSEMBLY

The 9-inch axle is most commonly used for high-performance street, racing, or off-road applications. To get the most out of this axle assembly, you need to select the ideal components, correctly perform the procedures in a clean environment, and accurately set up the differential. After all, you're going to transmit 400 or more horsepower through the axle.

You want it to be reliable and durable.

Many components and sub-assemblies make up the axle, so there is a huge benefit to laying out all the parts, taking your time, and being patient during the rebuild. Place all of the components on a bench to make certain that you have everything and have enough work space to get the job done. Take a few minutes to get things neat and organized, so the entire build goes easier, especially if this is your first project.

There is also a big benefit to doing the upfront research to get good parts from reputable vendors. If you can get Ford Motorsports products, you are a step ahead, but at times, the aftermarket is the only place to find items. This is especially true for most of the 9-inch axle parts nowadays.

This chapter details the assembly steps of a typical open differential followed by steps for assembling a Traction-Lok differential. To avoid redundancy, I skip certain portions of the Traction-Lok assembly process that are the same as for the open differential rebuild procedure.

The third-member assembly (with hypoid gear setup) and the axle housing assembly are also covered in this chapter.

"Gear case" is the term for the bare cast-iron center portion of the axle case that is installed from the front of the axle. When the unit is completely assembled with the gears, bearings, and differential it is referred to as the "third member" (see Chapter 5 for exploded views).

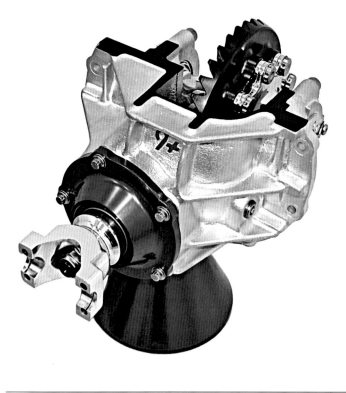

This cutaway display of an aftermarket Currie 9+ shows the nodular third member with the Daytona-style pinion cartridge. Even though this unit is a painted-up show piece, the quality of these units is extremely consistent and they offer superior performance.

Open-Differential Assembly

The differential pinions ride on pins, and the three pins are supported in the square center block. The three roll pins not only prevent the differential pinions from coming out, but also serve a secondary purpose of preventing the pins from rotating inside the differential housing.

With all of the parts clean and inventoried, the first order of business is to pre-lube all washers and gears using standard Type 2 grease. The grease serves a couple of purposes. It provides the much needed lubrication before the axle starts rotating and oils itself from splash.

The grease also serves as an assembly helper to hold the washers in place. Use a standard acid brush to spread the lithium-based assembly grease in place. Acid brushes typically have a tin or metal handle and are about 6 inches long. These are perfect for grease and other petroleum-based products because the handles do not become saturated as do typical wooden handles. Some plastic-handled brushes deteriorate over time when exposed to grease. Inexpensive acid brushes are found in your local hardware store's plumbing section as they are used for spreading flux prior to soldering copper plumbing.

Here are the internal components of the open differential. The four pinion gears provide added torque capacity. There are a total of six gears (two side gears and four pinion mates), and each has a washer between it and the differential housing. You may notice that these parts show no wear. Currie Enterprises reproduces the exact Ford replacement parts. These gears are made of the same or better material, so there really is no reason to re-use your old, worn-out parts with who knows how many miles on them.

1 Grease Pinion Surfaces

Use a standard acid brush to spread the lithium-based assembly grease on the pinion surfaces.

2 Grease Side Gears

Evenly spread a small dab of grease on the back surface of the side gears. This grease serves two purposes: to provide lubrication at initial running and to act as an assembly aid to hold the parts in place.

3 Install Pinion Washers

Apply a small amount of grease to the gears. Set the washers in place on the pinions. A grade 2 lithium-based grease with extreme pressure additives works perfectly for this and is readily available. Even Wal-Mart has it; just look for the National Lubrication Grease Institute (NLGI) grade 2 label on the tube.

4 Lay Down Washers

Put the side-gear washers in place. They are non-direction sensitive, so either side up is fine. Just make certain that all of the washers are installed and do not fall out during assembly.

5 Grease Top of Washers

Add a thin layer of grease on top of each washer.

6 Secure Differential

You can fabricate simple and helpful tools to hold components for the differential assembly. Here, the end of an old axle shaft has been cut off and welded to a chunk of steel plate. This is an 8.8-inch part, but the same can be made for a 9-inch.

Place the empty differential housing on the old axle shaft end and then into a vise. The 9-inch uses a two-piece differential (as compared to the single piece of the 8.8-inch differential), so you assemble the internal portion into the larger portion and then install the cover.

7 Install Side Gears

The first part to be installed is one of the side gears. Make sure that the washer is still in place on the back face so the gear and washer can be set in place in the bottom of the differential case.

Fully seat the gear all the way into the differential housing. Make sure to correctly line up the spline teeth.

8 Install Pinion Gears

Important!

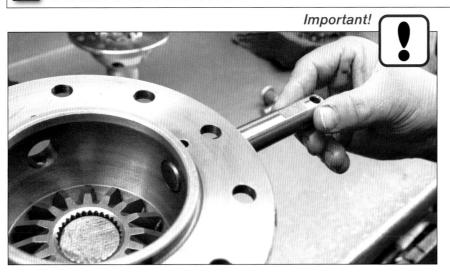

First, slide the long pin in by hand and only deep enough to hold it in place. Note that there are only three roll-pin holes in the differential case. These are spaced at 90 degrees and line up with the differential pin through the holes. The long pin goes in the middle of the three. Make sure to put the solid end in first. Ensure the differential pin stays below the differential case's inside diameter, so you can get the gear in place. Also, orient the pin so that the hole in the end lines up with the roll-pin hole in the differential housing. It will be vertical, as shown here.

Perform the same procedure for the two small pins. Have the long pin at the 6 o'clock position with the two smaller pins at 3 o'clock and 9 o'clock. Again, pay attention to the orientation of the roll-pin holes.

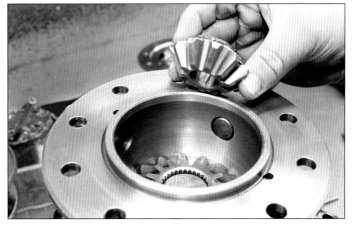

Install the differential pinion gears one at a time. Install the first gear on the long shaft. Make sure that the washer in still in place. Set the pinion in mesh with the side gear teeth and align it with the long pin shaft.

8 Install Pinion Gears CONTINUED

To hold the pinion gear in place, partially push the pin in (shown). Double-check that the washer is in place. Take care not to rotate the roll pin retention hole out of place. This is just a good practice to keep things aligned.

As always, check to make sure the pinion washers are in place. As before, ensure that the pinion teeth mesh with the side gear and partially install the pin to hold the pinion in place.

9 Install Rest of Pinions

Here is what the differential should look like with two of the pinions in place. The third and fourth pinions follow the same steps as above. The only unique part is that the third pinion temporarily rests in place without a shaft to support it.

10 Install Support Block

Once all four of the pinions are in place, the differential pins should support and hold three of them. Now install the differential gear and pin support block. Just set it in place on top of the side gear and align with the differential pinion shafts.

11 Make Sure Washers are Installed

Once installed, the support block should appear as shown. This is another good opportunity to look over all the pinions and make sure that the washers are in place. I have mentioned checking for the correct placement of the washers many times. Make sure they are installed. They are crucial for the correct operation and longevity of the unit.

12 Install Differential Pins

Make sure that the roll-pin hole is still positioned correctly and slide the long pin in place.

Slide the two short pins in place. Just as with the long pin, make sure to align the roll pins with the holes in the differential case.

To install the pins I use this modified center punch, but any standard punch or even a nail of the correct diameter works. Make sure that the differential pins are correctly lined up before you press in the roll pins. The roll pins can be a little tricky to remove if things aren't lined up, so take the extra time to be certain they are lined up. If the roll pin is not aligned correctly and the pin is partially driven in, it hits the differential pin and jams in place. Then pliers or some other means need to be used to remove the pin; typically this destroys the pin.

13 Install Roll Pins

The roll pins are an interference fit so they require some persuasion to get started and installed. They have a slight radius on the ends to help them compress into the holes. Begin to lightly tap the roll pins into place.

Continue to lightly tap the roll pins into place. Don't be too aggressive as you don't want to peen over the ends. Be careful to tap them straight down so they don't bend. Repeat this for all three pins. Do not drive them all the way down just yet. Note some gear oil in the differential case window (arrow). I use a combination of grease and a light coat of gear oil to hold the washer in place during assembly.

14 Make Pins Flush with Top Surface

Use your center punch to drive the pins. Proceed with light taps until all three pins are flush with the top surface.

15 Drive Pins into Place

Drive all three pins just a little below the top surface. This makes sure that they do not interfere with the mating cover.

16 Verify all Pins are in Place

Shown is a close-up of the roll pin just below the top surface. Also notice the pilot diameter has a slight chamfer to help you install the opposite case half.

17 Apply Grease to Pinions

Before installing the side gear, place a dab of assembly grease on all of the pinions.

18 Rotate Side and Pinion Gears

Give them a little roll as well to distribute some of the grease. I want to feel a smooth rolling motion and not a bumpy motion.

Set the other side gear in place. Since the pinions are aligned correctly from the bottom side gear, the second side gear just drops right in. It lines right up with the gear teeth of the four pinions.

19 Install Side Gears

20 Double-Check Washers

Make sure that the washer is in place and apply assembly grease to the face of the washer.

Carefully line up the differential case with the pilot diameter. Be sure the ring gear bolt holes line up at the same time. You may even want to use some ring gear bolts or pins to guide the two case halves together. Once you have done many of these, you will be able to do it by sight.

21 Close Case Halves

22 Install Side Cover

Once in place, lightly tap the center of the differential. You can use a dead-blow or plastic mallet (shown). You can also use a block of wood to protect the differential cover. Be careful to not dent or ding the bearing surface.

Here, the two halves are properly aligned and pressed completely together. There should be virtually no gap all the way around and even on the case split line as shown.

Traction-Lok Assembly

There are two limited-slip-style differentials available: the Equa Lok and the Traction-Lok. They are similar in design. The Equa Lok is quite rare because it was only used for a few years.

There are internal differences between the two and most parts are not interchangeable. The Equa Lok has four steel and three friction plates that are preloaded by a Belleville washer. The Traction-Lok has five steel and four friction plates. The first steel plate has friction material bonded to one side.

The assembly steps are very similar, except that you need to add a limited-slip clutch pack if you have a Traction-Lok differential. The clutch pack consists of clutch friction plates, steel reaction plates, and shims. This is very similar to the 8.8-inch assembly process, just with more pinion gears and a different preload spring arrangement.

Here are the internal components of the Traction-Lok differential assembly. On the left, you can see gears similar to those for the open differential, but there are some additional pieces. These are the clutch plate inner carrier, differential case cover with four unique slots machined in place, clutch pack, shims, and springs.

Some wear caps for the clutch plates are also used on the stock and nodular-iron units of this differential case. (Some of the newer aftermarket billet-style covers may not use these caps, but all others do.) Also, there are two different side gears: one with a pilot feature on the back surface and one with a flat surface.

1 Apply Grease to Pinions

Apply assembly grease to the back of the pinions, to the side gears, and to the washers to help keep them in place.

2 Install Side Gear in Differential Case

Install the same spline tool in the vise as shown in step 6 on page 72 for an open differential. Put the differential case in place and load in the first side gear with its washer in place. This is the side gear with the shoulder on the back surface.

3 Partially Assemble Differential

This part of the assembly follows the procedure for the open differential (see steps 8 and 9 on pages 73 and 74). Make sure that you have all the pinion washers in place.

4 Install Differential Support Block

Install the differential pin support block, which has four small holes in the corners. This block is symmetrical and does not require any special orientation.

5 Install Differential Pins

Install and align the three differential pins, which is just a matter of pushing them in place by hand (see step 12 on page 75). Don't forget to double-check the alignment of the roll-pin holes.

6 Install Roll Pins

Install and fully seat the three roll pins (see steps 14 through 17 on pages 76 and 77). Take extra care to not dent or ding the pilot diameter surfaces. Note that this pilot diameter is countersunk, as opposed to being a raised surface as with the open differential.

7 Install Preload Springs

Here you can see that all of the pinion washers are in place. The three roll pins have been tapped in just below the mounting surface. Now you need to install the preload springs for the clutch pack in the bores of the differential pin block. Dip each one in assembly lube before you drop it in place (left). Repeat until you have all four springs in place (right).

8 Grease Pinions

Add another dab of the grease on the visible end of each spring. Add some grease to all four pinions, rotate to feel for smooth motion, and perform a final check to be sure that all springs and washers are in place.

9 Install Spring Plate

Add the spring plate. Orient it so that the arched cutouts line up with the long differential pin. The long pin is the one that has only a single roll pin on the axis (the one in the middle of the three pins).

10 Apply Grease

Fully seat the spring support plate. Add a thin layer of assembly grease on the back of this plate with an acid brush.

Clutch Pack Sub-Assembly

1 Inspect Clutch Pack Components

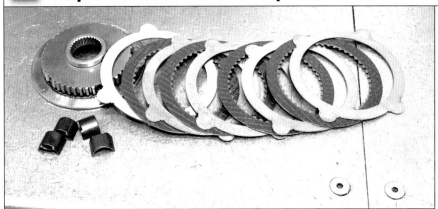

The clutch pack components are laid out in order of assembly along with the steel wear plates. I recommend pre-soaking the clutch plates in friction modifier for at least 30 minutes prior to assembly.

2 Pre-Lube Clutch Carrier

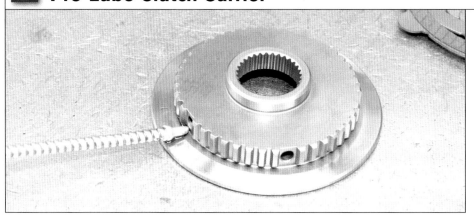

The next step in working on the clutch pack sub-assembly is to pre-lube the clutch inner plate carrier. You can use common gear oil for this.

3 Install Reaction Plates

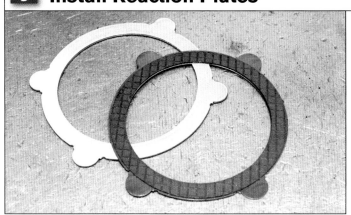 

The tabbed outer reaction plate has friction material on a single side (left). Most people refer to this as the composite plate. The four tabs fit into the mating slots in the differential case. Install the first reaction plate with the friction surface down, which is in contact with the inner plate carrier (right).

4 Install Friction Plates

The friction plates have friction material on both sides, so there is no concern as to which side is installed up. These plates have the mating teeth in their inside diameter and line up with the teeth on the inner plate carrier.

5 Install Steel Reaction Plates

The reaction plates are plain steel. Continue to build up the clutch pack alternating between steel reaction plates and friction plates. There are four steel plates, four friction plates, and one unique composite plate, which has friction material on only one side.

6 Finish Clutch Pack Buildup

When you have the entire clutch and reaction plate pack correctly assembled, the sub-assembly should look just like this. The top plate is a steel tabbed-style reaction plate.

7 Install Four Reaction Plate Wear Caps

These stop the tabbed plates from wearing into the softer cast iron of the original Ford castings that are soft compared to aftermarket units. The five missing teeth on the inner clutch plate carrier are oil transfer holes. This feature allows oil into the clutch pack to help lubricate the pack. More importantly, it transfers heat from the plates to the incoming fresh oil.

8 Apply Grease to Clutch Plate Carrier

The final preparation step of the clutch pack sub-assembly is to apply a small amount of assembly grease to the top surface of the clutch plate carrier. Use an acid brush to apply a thin layer. This grease helps hold the parts in place.

9 Install Inner Plate Carrier Washer

The inner plate carrier washer goes on the top of the assembled clutch pack sub-assembly.

Differential Cover Assembly

1 Install Outer Carrier Plate

2 Install Shim

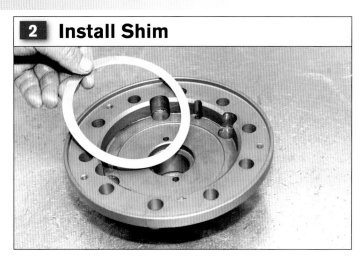

If your parts are used or have signs of burrs, smooth them out with an emery cloth or a small file, then thoroughly clean the plate. Any of this abrasive material in the oil and clutch pack will surely cause parts to fail prematurely. Apply a small amount of gear oil to the raised surface as shown. This is the surface that the shim rides on.

Add a small amount of gear oil in the shim pocket. Just a thin coating is all that is required; too much oil changes the assembled clutch pack height. Set the shim in place. This is the shim that may require adjustment if the clutch pack height is not correct. Unfortunately, to adjust this shim, means disassembling the unit and replacing the shim.

3 Install Clutch Pack and Inner Plate Carrier

Place the clutch pack and inner plate carrier into the differential cover. Note that steel caps on the tabs are not used because the new Currie differential housings are made out of nodular iron, which is much stronger than the original Ford production pieces and therefore do not require the wear caps.

4 Oil Clutch Pack and Inner Plate Carrier

Add some gear oil to the recessed surface. The side gear back face is in contact with this surface during operation.

5 Set Side Gear into Position

Place the side gear in the pre-oiled recess with the toothed side up. The design of this flat back surface is unique to the Traction-Lok differential. This completes the differential cover assembly process.

Case Halves Assembly

1 Gather all Components

I have found that it is best to place the cover assembly on the bench and carefully set the main differential housing on top of it. The grease on the main components side of the differential acts as an assembly aid to keep things together.

Pay special attention to the three through holes on the main case because you need them to align with the small threaded holes on the cover. Here, these holes are on the same flange surface as the ring gear bolt holes (but have a larger diameter). You can see them at approximately 2, 7, and 10 o'clock.

2 Bolt Differential Halves Together

Once you have the two halves together and the bolt holes line up, bolt them together. Use three countersunk head-style bolts for this. Get all of the bolts started and then tighten them snugly in place.

3 Press Case Halves Together

Since the clutch pack is preloaded, use a press to overcome that preload and press the two case halves together. While still in the press, tighten the three bolts securely. Using a press really makes this step simple as it can be easy to strip the Allen-head bolts depending on the amount of clutch pack preload.

Torque Fasteners, Special Tool

4 Check Preload

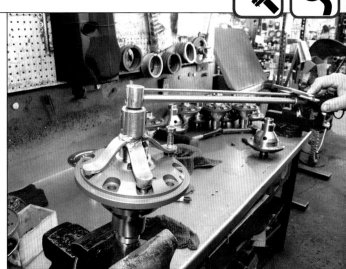

Check the preload torque and make adjustments to the shim as required. The nominal shim is .050 inch thick. This homemade tool (left) is made from an old socket along with steel straps and bolts. Depending on the application, the preload torque is between 100 and 250 ft-lbs for new plates. This is a wide range but the torque may fluctuate by as much as 40 ft-lbs.

The tool is designed to straddle the bearing journal on the differential case (right) and allow you to rotate the differential case through the ring gear bolt holes. Use a torque wrench to check the preload (or break-away torque) of the clutch pack along with the torque required to keep the gear moving steadily. You want a running torque value of 75 ft-lbs for used plates and 155 to 195 ft-lbs for new plates. If it's too tight, the tires skid during turn events and if it's too loose, you may have the dreaded single-wheel peel before the gear-separating force comes into play.

5 Align Side Gear and Inner Plate Carrier

Line up the side gear and inner plate carrier because these have separate splines. This photo shows the splines out of position, making it impossible to install the axle shaft later.

6 Index Teeth for Alignment

This photo shows that I have indexed the unit to have the teeth perfectly in alignment. Although this is a very simple step, it's often overlooked. Of course, if it is forgotten, you can just slightly rotate the axle shaft on the opposite side relative to the ring gear, but you must install the other axle shaft first. It is much easier to do it now. Also, if you forget about this, you may be tempted to draw in the axle shaft with the T-bolts, and that creates a huge problem.

Third-Member Assembly

This is where you combine the assembled differential with the gear case and hypoid gears. Plus, you also add the necessary bearings, seals, and shims.

You can purchase individual pieces or a complete kit that includes everything that you need.

Use the large shims on the left to make pinion mounting distance adjustments. The bearings just below them are the differential case bearings. The bearings at the upper right are the pinion straddle mount, head, and tail bearings with the solid shims and retainer next to that. The rest of the pieces are miscellaneous seals, pinion nut, gear marking compound, and thread sealant.

1 Inspect Component Kit

2 Lay Out Parts

Important!

 Make sure that everything is accounted for and that everything is clean and prepped for final assembly. Notice that I have already pressed in the pinion bearing races in the pinion cartridge.

3 Install Differential Bearings

PRO TIP *Press the differential bearing onto the differential case. It is a press fit, so you can use a hydraulic press (shown) or an arbor press. Make sure that you install the bearing in the correct orientation. The smaller diameter should point toward the outside of the differential. Be careful to only press on the bearing inner race. I like to use an actual inner race where the cage and rollers have been removed. This is where it is nice to save old, damaged bearing races, as they make perfect press tools.*

4 Start Ring Gear Installation

The hypoid ring gear has a slight press fit and is held in place with ten bolts.

5 Apply Thread Locker to Ring Gear Bolts

Use solvent and brush to thoroughly clean the threads of the bolts and ring gear holes. You want to ensure that all oil and debris have been removed. Apply thread sealant (Loctite) to the first few threads of the ring gear bolts. This is an important step because you do not want a ring gear bolt to come loose inside the axle. For added insurance, you can even add a small amount of sealant to the ring gear bolt holes. (This goes for all Loctite joints.)

6 Place Differential Case over Ring Gear

Place some red thread sealant in the ring gear bolt holes. The ring gear is not oriented or clocked in any special way to the differential case. Make sure that the holes are lined up.

7 Install Ring Gear

By hand, pull the ring gear into position and install a couple of bolts. Begin by starting two bolts that are opposite each other to hold the gear in place. The bolts have washers under the heads. These smaller-headed bolts with washers are used in Traction-Lok applications only. Open differentials and most other aftermarket differentials use larger-headed ring gear bolts.

8 Install Ring Gear Bolts

Continue partially threading in the remaining bolts. By starting all of the bolts loosely, it helps to make sure that the ring gear is guided correctly onto the differential case. Snug all of the bolts. There is no need to get them tight as the differential case is not securely anchored on the bench and just twists all over.

9 Set Differential in Spline Tool

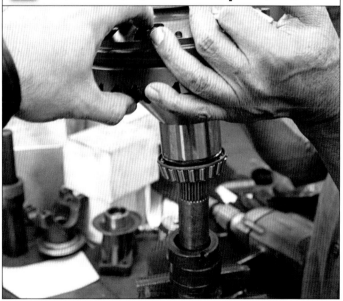

In order to hold the differential case in place while you torque the ring gear bolts, use the homemade spline tool in a bench vise. Clamp the tool in the bench vise and set the differential in place. Make sure that the spline is engaged in the differential side gear.

10 Secure Differential in Vise

 *You can make a homemade T-shaped tool by taking some old pieces of axle shaft splines and welding them to a bar. I will insert this into the other side gear. Now you can hold the side gear in place while you torque ring gear bolts. While this may seem like overkill, it is an effective technique rather than trying to clamp the differential case in the vise. Clamping the case in a vise is not recommended and usually leaves gouges and stress risers, which could lead to cracking and failure.*

11 Torque Ring Gear Bolts

Torque the ring gear bolts while keeping the differential from rotating. Torque them in stages to a final torque of 65 ft-lbs. You can also use a staggered star pattern to evenly draw up the gear. Take your time and do this in steps so you do not pull on the gear unevenly and risk any misalignment and potential warping or gear runout.

12 Install Pinion Gear

Unlike the 8.8-inch pinion, the 9-inch style utilizes a removable pinion cartridge. This cast pinion cartridge allows you the freedom to adjust pinion mounting depth independent of bearing preload. So the pinion head bearing installs without a shim underneath it.

The pinion head bearing is a press fit. Using a hydraulic press, press the bearing all the way down until it contacts the machined ledge on the pinion back face. As with the differential bearings, make sure to only press on the inner race of the bearings and not the cage.

12 Install Pinion Gear *CONTINUED*

Once the bearing has been fully seated, install the solid shim (left). You can upgrade to a solid shim instead of the collapsible spacer for a stiffer bearing arrangement. There are advantages and disadvantages to the solid spacer approach. The main disadvantage is that you may have to change the shim a few times to achieve the correct preload. But once you have it, there is a solid connection between the bearings. Once the spacer is in place, start out with a .012-inch shim. On the right, the shim is hanging on the spline but it needs to go all the way down the pinion shaft and line up with the solid spacer.

13 Set Pinion Tail Bearing into Pinion Cartridge

Do not add any assembly lube at this time. The new Timken bearings feature a rust preventative and lubricant. This lubricant is required for accurate torque-to-turn measurements, so you do not want to remove this lubricant or add any oil or grease.

14 Install Pinion Cartridge

Install the pinion cartridge with its bearings in place on the pinion. This is just a matter of carefully setting the partially assembled casting on the pinion shaft with the inner surface facing toward the pinion head.

The entire pinion shaft with cartridge looks like this.

15 Press In Pinion Tail Bearing

While you still have a load on the assembly, rotate the cartridge and feel for the correct torque-to-turn. If you don't have experience doing this, you just need to install the flange and nut, then you can measure the torque-to-turn while holding the pinion cartridge in a vise.

Precision Measurement

16 Test Torque of Pinion Assembly

For new bearings, target a torque-to-turn in the range of 13 to 15 in-lbs. For used bearings, the amount is about 7 in-lbs. If the torque-to-turn measurement is lower than the specifications, reduce the overall shim stack height. On the other hand, if the torque-to-turn is too high, add more shims to increase the overall shim height.

17 Install Pinion Seal

Now that the correct pinion bearing preload has been reached and verified by torque-to-turn measurements, it's time to install the pinion seal. Before driving the seal into place, make sure that it is not tipped.

Special Tool

17 **Install Pinion Seal** *CONTINUED*

Use an appropriate-size seal driver and exercise care to make sure that the seal stays aligned correctly (above left). Once in place the seal lip should not have any gaps all the way around. The blue line (above right) is the seal lip between the driver tool and the cartridge.

Before installing the pinion flange, apply a small amount of grease to the seal surface of the pinion yoke, so the seal is never dry and doesn't burn up prior to adequate lube getting to it. This is just for the initial assembly.

18 Seat Yoke onto Pinion Shaft

Use a shop press to fully seat the yoke. A slight helix or twist is on the pinion splines to take up any backlash. This makes the yoke a press fit on the pinion. Note the solid spacer shim on the press plate; it was extra from the installation kit.

19 Install Pinion Nut

The last part to be installed is the pinion nut. Thread locker and sealant (orange) comes pre-applied on the nut threads and the bottom flange surface. These materials help prevent oil from slowly seeping under the nut. This is another reason to use a new nut each time. If you have the solid spacer arrangement (shown) and it is already shimmed correctly, just tighten the nut with an impact gun. Shoot for about 220 ft-lbs of torque.

20 Install O-Ring

This O-ring goes in the groove on the cast cartridge. It is partially installed here; you want to chase the O-ring into the groove all the way around. Make sure that it is fully seated and not twisted.

21 Install Pinion Bearing

Install the pinion straddle mount bearing. This roller bearing fits into the main gear case. Install it through the pinion cartridge hole. Gently set it in place and then fully seat it with the appropriate-diameter press tool and a few taps with a hammer on the outer race.

22 Set Bearing Retainer in Place

The metal tabbed retainer keeps this bearing in its pocket. Set it in place and use a driver tool to seat the tabs (left). Take your time and make sure that the wider of the tabs are locked into the groove in the third-member casting (right).

23 Apply Assembly Grease

Important!

24 Install Pinion Cartridge !

Apply some assembly grease on the pinion cartridge O-ring surface. This makes sure that the O-ring doesn't get damaged during installation of the cartridge.

! Start with a nominal pinion shim of about .014 inch. To verify the shim is correct, the ring and pinion set needs to be installed and torqued in place. Then perform a pattern check. Torque down all the parts and do another pattern check.

24 Install Cartridge *CONTINUED*

Make certain that the cartridge is oriented correctly. Temporarily install the bolts. These bolts may need to be removed later to adjust the pinion cartridge shim. Even if the shim is correct, you still remove these bolts later to apply thread locker. If the shim is not correct, then the bolts and cartridge need to be carefully removed and the shim replaced. The final torque specification for these bolts is 35 ft-lbs.

25 Install Differential Unit

Flip the gear case and set the races in place between the threaded portion of the gear case. Install the differential case with its bearings and races in place.

26 Set Adjuster Nuts

Set the adjuster nuts in place. Take extra care to make sure that the threads are lined up correctly.

27 Tighten Adjuster Nuts

Lightly tighten the adjuster nuts. This is just to get things started. You really can't go much beyond finger tight as the top of the bearing cap is not in place yet. (Here you see my homemade tool, but similar production tools are also available.)

28 Install Bearing Caps

Apply some thread sealant to the bearing cap bolts (left) and install them (right). Be very careful to make sure that the cap lines up with the adjuster nut threads and tighten the bolts in place. Don't forget to check that you set the correct caps as marked previously for left and right. Torque to 80 ft-lbs.

Precision Measurement

29 Set Ring Gear Backlash

Use a dial indicator with a magnetic base. Line up the dial indicator with the outside diameter of the gear tooth and zero the gauge. Look for .010 to .016 inch for OEM gears and .007 to .010 inch for aftermarket gears. For used gears, aim for .010. (If in doubt, contact your gear vendor.)

The adjuster nuts are really helpful to move the ring gear back and forth. Unlike the 8.8-inch axle that requires unique shims every time, just loosen one side and tighten the opposite side to move the gear.

TECH TIP

Properly Tighten Adjuster Nuts

The adjuster nut has 16 threads per inch, which translates to 16 full turns for the nut to travel an axial distance of 1 inch. That is 5,760 degrees of rotation for 1 inch of travel. There are 12 notches in the adjuster nut, which is one every 30 degrees. If you divide the 30 degrees by

5,760 degrees, you get .005-inch difference of axial travel per notch. So, if you have everything set up correctly, you always want to advance to the next notch before installing the anti-rotation tab. ∎

30 Apply Gear-Marking Compound

Apply gear-marking compound to a few of the gear teeth and check the pattern. (Pattern-setting details are discussed in Chapter 7.) If the pattern needs to be adjusted, remove the differential, adjust the pinion cartridge shim, and reset the ring gear backlash. Then check the pattern again.

This can be tedious but is crucial to a quiet and durable axle. To achieve this pattern, I had to change the pinion cartridge shim three different times, but this is typical. This required me to remove the pinion cartridge bolts and cartridge assembly from the gear case in order to exchange the shim for a different thickness. I put white gear-marking compound on about seven teeth and regular, old, brown assembly lube grease on about three teeth because the brown makes a more identifiable footprint onto the white compound. I rotated the pinion and provided drag on the ring gear with my other hand to achieve the contact pattern.

31 Install Adjuster Keepers

Secure the adjuster nuts. Typically the retainer clips and adjuster nut do not line up. Always tighten the adjuster nut into the bearing cap. The bearings should be preloaded and not in clearance. Apply thread sealant to the retainer clip screws, make sure the the steel clip is lined up, and then install the screws.

32 Torque Down Retainer Clips

Lightly tap the retainer clips to make sure that the tang is in place. Torque the retainer clip screws to 20 ft-lbs. Remove the pinion cartridge bolts one last time to apply thread sealant. Only remove and apply to one bolt at a time because you don't want the pinion to come loose. Torque the pinion cartridge bolts to 35 ft-lbs.

Axle Housing Assembly

You're at the point in the process where the differential has been completely assembled. Also, the third member has been completely assembled with the hypoid gears, bearings, and differential. Now you can proceed to the axle housing assembly process. Once you get the housing prepped, you can install the third member.

Third-Member Installation

1 Double-Check Axle Lengths (if custom)

If you want to use a custom-width axle, the shop that fabricates the unit needs to take some final measurements to make sure all dimensions are correct.

The homemade fixture is set in place to replicate the differential pin retainer block (left). A magnet has been epoxied to the inside of the case, which is a great idea to keep any debris from circulating through the axle. Then a set of fixtures is installed on the wheel-end side of the housing, along with the axle shafts. Once everything is in place a slight clearance from the end of the axle shafts and the fixture should be present (right). Of course, the overall axle width, shock and spring brackets, and any other bracketry are all checked dimensionally and compared to the custom build sheet.

If you are rebuilding an axle and you've already verified the dimensions, none of this is required.

2 Apply RTV

Apply a bead of black RTV on the axle housing and make sure to circle the studs. Then set the paper gasket in place and follow with an additional bead of RTV.

3 Install Third Member

Carefully lower the third member in place. It weighs 85 pounds, so it requires some strength to handle and install. If you're not comfortable installing it yourself, have a helper give you a hand. The studs are a great to help align the unit but you still want to set it in place slowly and carefully.

4 Install Washers

From the factory, copper washers were placed underneath the nuts for the third member. Most of the time, the original copper washers are long gone but you do want a soft material under these nuts (left). In the aftermarket, aluminum washers are an easy and common replacement. The third member is just a rough casting and not machined or spot faced under these fasteners. The soft washer conforms to the raw casting variations. You can also use nylon-style lock nuts, just to be safe (right). Torque these ten nuts in a crisscross pattern in stages. First snug them all in place, then torque to 20 ft-lbs, and finally to 40 ft-lbs.

Of course, one telltale sign that you have a 9-inch axle is that the bottom third-member nuts cannot be accessed with a socket. For these you have to use an open-style wrench and your judgment on the correct feel of the final torque.

5 Replace Wheel Studs

If you have new axle shafts, the studs are not typically installed. Even if you are going to use old axle shafts, replacing the studs with fresh ones is a good idea. This is a unique press that was made just to push the studs in place. You can achieve the same arrangement with a socket on the bottom side of the axle shaft and using a hammer to seat the stud. Just be careful and make sure that the stud is driven in straight. Some aftermarket axle shafts have threaded-in studs, which makes this step very easy.

6 Inspect Axle Shaft

The finished axle shaft with the studs in place should look like this. Note the hole on the top of the flange. This is the access hole for the axle shaft retainer nuts.

7 Install Wheel Bearing Parts

For a typical, sealed, large bearing wheel end retention you install the bearing retaining plate on the axle shaft first with the disc brake spacing lip pointing up. Then install the sealed ball bearing and the lock ring (if applicable). You need to press the lock ring and bearing all the way down to the positive stop on the axle shaft. This requires a fair amount of press force.

8 Install Bearing and Lock Ring

Place the components in a hydraulic press and press them together (left). Use a spacer under the lock ring and on top of the axle shaft for support and to press against. Once fully seated, the shaft should look like this (right). The retainer plate is trapped on the shaft now but free to float around until it is bolted to the axle housing.

9 Install Seal into Axle Housing

In small or large bearing wheel-end applications, when a sealed ball bearing is being utilized, install the seal into the axle housing end (left). These seals keep the gear oil in the axle tube and contaminants out, but the bearing seals do not necessarily keep hot gear oil from passing the seal. If you are using the sealed ball style of wheel bearing, don't forget this step and make sure that the seal is installed straight and fully seated (right).

10 Apply Grease on Seal

Place a coat of lithium-based grease on the seal as well as on the inside of the housing ends (left). This helps lubricate the seal during initial running and helps the axle slide in place. For good measure, also apply grease to the seal running surface on the axle shaft (right).

11 Install T-Shaped Bolts

Four T-shaped bolts go into the axle flange (left). Because they are T-shaped, they do not rotate when you tighten the nuts on the other side. These bolts hold the brake backing plate and axle retainer plate in place (right).

Important!

12 Install Brake Backing Plate

Install the brake backing plate and thread in the bolts loosely hold it in place (left). This hardware is for a typical aftermarket disc brake arrangement with a combined parking brake inside the rotor. These brake shoes are cable actuated, and that's why you don't see a hydraulic wheel cylinder. Apply some grease on the seal surface of the axle shaft (to aid in installation) then carefully install the axle shaft (right). Be very careful to support the axle and not drag the spline over the seal surface.

Professional Mechanic Tip, Torque Fasteners

13 Align Axle Shaft with Differential Splines

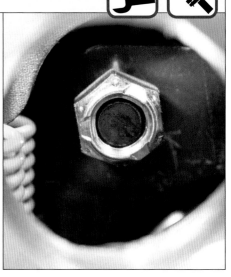

The axle shaft splines may be a little tricky to get aligned in the differential side. Take your time and tip the shaft until the splines line up. You may have to lightly tap the axle shaft to fully seat the splines. Then reach through the access hole in the axle flange to line up the retainer plate with the bolts (left). This is tricky as bolts can fall back out. Once you have them lined up, install the four nuts (middle). Tighten the 3/8-inch torque prevailing nuts to 35 ft-lbs (right). Repeat this procedure for the opposite side.

14 Install Wheel End Bearings

The assembly process for a tapered-roller, big-bearing wheel end is similar to that of a ball-bearing style, but there are a couple of differences. The tapered-roller, big-bearing style is not sealed but shares the oil with the axle. Do not install a seal in the axle housing or the bearing will be starved of oil.

The bearing comes pre-assembled (left) with a pre-lubed bearing and seal as one unit plus the axle-retaining ring. These take the place of a ball bearing. There is still a retention plate and in some cases, a brake specific spacer ring is required on the axle shaft. So when you install these on the axle shaft, they go in the following order: retaining plate, spacer ring, seal/bearing (with seal toward the spacer ring), and retaining ring. The right photo shows the bearing/seal assembly taken apart.

The seal outside diameter is a slip-fit in the axle housing end and when you tighten the T-bolts in place, it draws the whole assembly into a preloaded condition. This preload causes the outer diameter of the seal to expand and seal into the housing. This is a very robust wheel end bearing, but it's tricky to disassemble. You can re-use the seal, but be very careful when getting the already expanded outside diameter in the housing. If you need to replace the seal, it is best to replace the entire bearing unit.

15 Install Brake Rotor

Finally, set the brake rotor and caliper in place (left). An aftermarket disc setup is shown here, but the steps are very similar for a drum-style arrangement. I recommend applying thread sealant to the caliper bolts before they are installed (right).

RING AND PINION ASSEMBLY

Many parts compose a rear axle and its most important function is to provide torque multiplication and speed reduction. This is accomplished with a right-angle drive gear arrangement called a hypoid gear set. The next most important aspect of the axle is to split torque to the wheels through a differential.

This chapter explores two of the most common manufacturing methods of hypoid gears: face-hobbed (or two-cut) and face-milled (or five-cut). It's important to have an understanding of these two types because the pattern moves differently and at different rates depending on the type of manufacturing. More simply stated, if you try to shim the position of a face-milled gear using the face-hobbed process, you won't achieve the correct position and gear contact pattern. The same is true for shimming a face-hobbed gear with a face-milled approach. Therefore, you need to accurately select the right process for the right gear.

Many people have selected the wrong process, even some who have been building axles for years. Making this mistake can be very frustrating because the assembly is suddenly noisy.

Face hobbing is a continuous indexing process in which the gear tooth surfaces are machined while both the cutter and the gear are rotating. The two machining steps are ring gear roughing and finishing and pinion roughing and finishing. One machine is required per step.

Face milling is a single indexing process in which one gear tooth slot is machined at a time. In effect, the part is stationary while the cutter rotates. Two machines and two processes are needed to produce the gear:

This is a typical ring and pinion from the 8.8-inch axle along with bearing, collapsible spacer, and pinion. The ring-and-pinion gear determines the gear ratio of the rear axle assembly, and therefore the gear ratio directly impacts vehicle acceleration and fuel economy. In addition, the face-hobbed and face-milled gears require different setup procedures, which are covered in this chapter.

Actual Gear Tooth

Stretched Gear Tooth

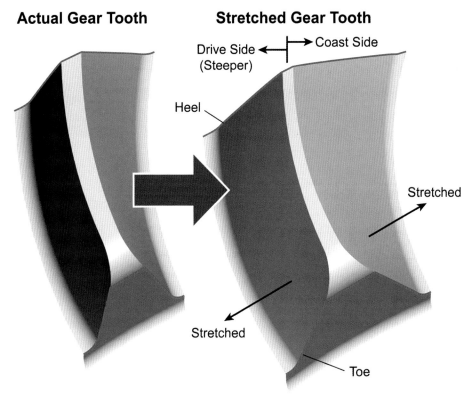

This computer-generated ring gear tooth illustrates gear patterns better than actual hardware. The tooth profile on the left is the correct shape. The one on the right has been stretched to make it easier to see pattern changes. The outside diameter of the ring gear is referred to as the heel of the gear. The inside diameter is referred to as the toe of the gear. The convex (or bowed) surface of the gear tooth is the drive side. The concave (or curved in) side is the coast side.

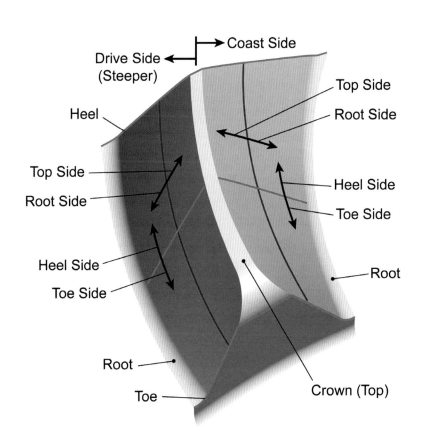

The blue lines divide the gear face between the heel and toe portions. The red lines divide the gear between root and crown portions.

The root is the valley between the gear teeth; the crown is the top surface of the tooth, which is sometimes called the top land or flank.

Ideally, you want the pattern centered on the tooth face between the root and the crown, and also between the heel and the toe. In other words, you want the pattern to be at the intersection of the blue and red lines in this illustration.

For high-performance applications, I favor the pattern being toward the toe portion of the tooth, so the entire gear-mounting system deflects (the pattern does not run off the tooth). This tighter pattern does have a slight noise disadvantage, which is generally acceptable for high-performance applications.

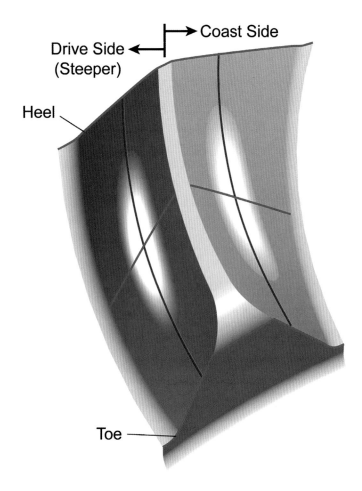

Drive Side (Steeper)
Coast Side
Heel
Toe

This illustration shows the ideal bench pattern contact. You cannot always achieve this because of several factors, including housing machining tolerances, gear manufacturing, etc.

You should always strive to have the pattern centered between the root and top surfaces of the gear. So you want the pattern to sit on the red line even if the pattern has to be closer to the heel or toe.

The main factor for centering the pattern on the red line is the pinion mounting distance. If you are setting up a used gear set, focus more on the coast side as this surface has less wear on it and is a better indicator of gear position.

Remove the used gear set to take contact pattern and backlash measurements. If the gear is quiet and works well in the vehicle and is only being changed to get a different ratio, for example, it is beneficial to have these measurements to act as a guide for re-assembly into a different housing later.

gear roughing both drive and coast sides and gear finishing both drive and coast sides.

The pinion requires three machines and three operations: roughing both drive and coast surfaces, finishing the drive side, and finishing the coast side.

Both types of gears are lapped together as a set and their ring and pinion must stay together. The ring/ pinion set and the differential bearing caps must stay matched in the axle.

All new Ford 8.8-inch original equipment and Ford Racing gears are face hobbed. Face-hobbed gears offer huge benefits from manufacturing and product strength standpoints, which is why the newer Ford 8.8-inch gears have switched to this process.

All Ford 9-inch gears (original equipment and aftermarket) and 8.8-inch aftermarket gears are face milled. (See my other CarTech book, *High-Performance Differentials, Axles and Drivelines,* for more details on both types.)

There are two reasons that the 9-inch gears are never face hobbed. The first is that the cutter path for face hobbing does not clear the straddle mount pinion on the 9-inch-style pinion head. (However, there are engineering solutions to resolve this.) Second, aftermarket gear producers have already installed the necessary manufacturing equipment for face milling. The machine cost to install face-hobbing equipment can quickly reach $2 million, and the typical aftermarket company cannot charge or sell enough gears to realistically recoup this initial capital expense.

Note that I do not cover ring gear spacers or different "series" of differential cases because they do not pertain to Ford 8.8-inch or 9-inch axles. General Motors and other axle manufacturers use a different ring gear mounting distance based on ratio and, therefore, sometimes require unique differential cases when changing ratios. In contrast, the Ford axle differential case can work with nearly any ratio, which simplifies determining a suitable case for a rebuild. When the ratio starts to get numerically high, above 4.56:1, there may be some unique things required to install the gear set. This is not typical for car tires but can be common for off-road trucks or trucks with large-diameter tires.

Face-Hobbed Gears

These include OE and replacement 8.8-inch gears.

This computer model of the ring gear tooth face illustrates a face-hobbed tooth form. Note that the tooth profile has a uniform depth across the entire face.

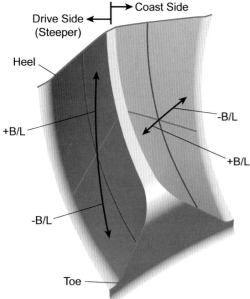

You want to have the pattern centered, and this diagram illustrates certain shift patterns. Changes in backlash (B/L) for a face-hobbed gear set are shown. Notice that the black arrows represent backlash increasing or decreasing. As backlash increases the pattern shifts toward the top of the tooth surface. The direction and slope of the arrows shows that the pattern moves slower up the tooth on the drive side as compared to the coast side. Also, the pattern moves faster from heel to toe with backlash changes on the drive side. This makes it easiest to concentrate on the drive side of the pattern, as the coast-side pattern moves slower with backlash changes.

On Ford OE and replacement gears, face-hobbed ring gears do not have the tapered back face machined. Here, you can see the area between the differential case mounting flange and the ring gear teeth. Close inspection reveals that the beveled surface is rough and has been left as an as-forged surface. This is an obvious sign of the type of process that was used to produce the gear—face hobbing. (On a factory face-milled gear, this surface is machined.)

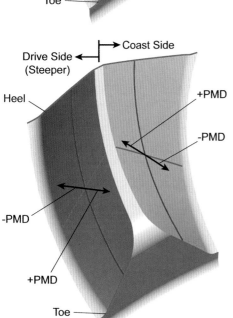

This diagram illustrates how the pattern shifts with changes in the pinion mounting distance (PMD). The PMD is changed with the pinion head shim for the 8.8-inch axle (the 9-inch axle uses the pinion cartridge shim). As you increase the PMD, which is accomplished with a thinner shim, the pattern shifts closer to the top face on the drive and coast surfaces. At the same time, the pattern shifts toward the toe on the drive surface of the tooth and toward the heel on the coast surface.

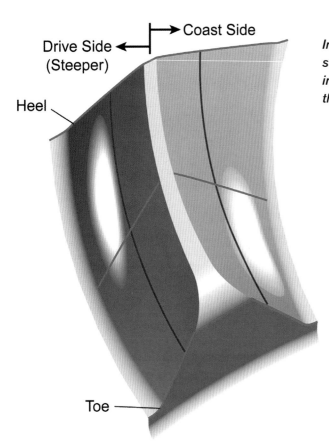

In this diagram, the pattern is toward the heel and root on the drive surface and toward the toe and root on the coast surface. Decreasing the pinion shim thickness allows you to move the pattern toward the top of the tooth.

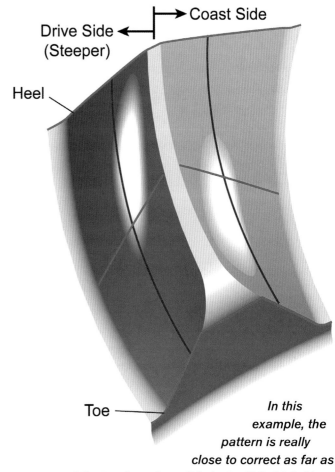

In this example, the pattern is really close to correct as far as root to top of the tooth surface; it is just a little high. You just need to center it between heel and toe on each surface. Decreasing the backlash corrects this pattern.

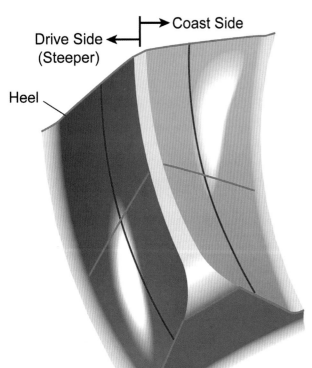

Here, the pattern is toward the toe on the drive surface and toward the heel on the coast surface. The pattern is also a little low, or closer to the root on both surfaces. Increasing the backlash corrects this pattern.

Face-Milled Gears

These include all 9-inch, after-market 8.8-inch, and early OE 8.8-inch gears.

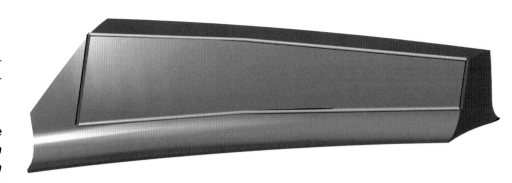

This is a computer model of the face-milled tooth profile. Based on the manufacturing process, the tooth profile has a varying tooth depth from the inside of the gear to the outside.

The tapered-tooth depth of a face-milled profile can be measured, but it is also visually apparent. The tooth depth varies from just over .500 inch to under .300 inch from one end to the other. This is relevant so you understand the correct method to shim the gear position and subsequent bench contact pattern.

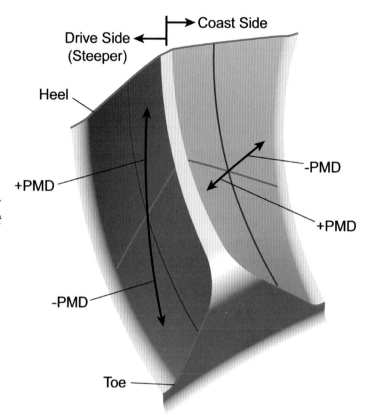

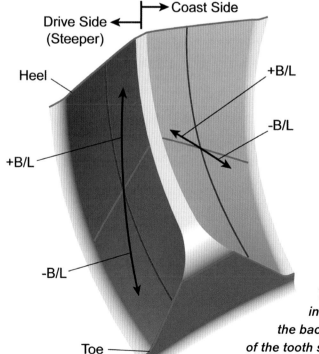

With a face-milled gear, an increase in PMD moves the pattern toward the heel and top of the tooth surface on the drive side. It moves the pattern toward the toe and top surface of the tooth on the coast side. To achieve this increase in PMD, you need to decrease the pinion shim thickness.

The pattern for a face-milled gear must be centered at the intersection of the blue and red lines on the tooth surfaces. As the backlash is increased, the pattern shifts toward the heel and top of the tooth surface on the drive side and shifts slower in the same direction on the coast side. Based on the pattern shifting quicker on the drive side, that is where it is easier to see subtle changes.

This pinion was originally set up with the carryover shim thickness of .026 inch. The pattern is biased toward the heel and top of the tooth surface on the drive side. If you install a .030-inch pinion shim, the pattern shifts perfectly.

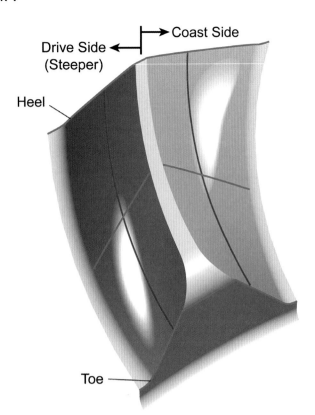

This diagram shows a pinion head shim that is too thick and a pinion mounting distance that is too short. The pattern is too close to the root and toe surfaces on the drive side and biased toward the heel on the coast side.

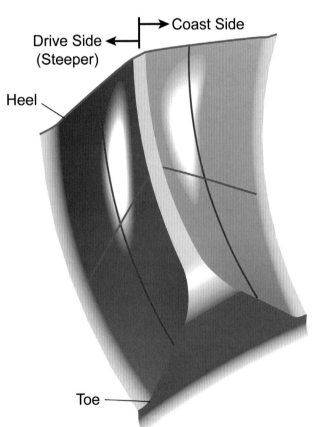

This pattern is biased toward the heel and top surfaces on drive and coast. All you need to do is reduce the gear backlash and this pattern should align itself perfectly.

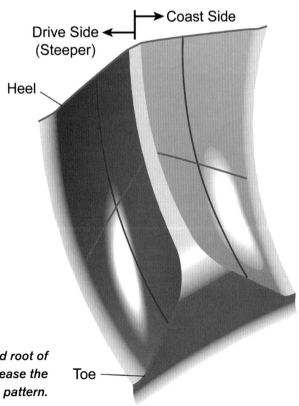

In this illustration, you see a pattern biased toward the toe and root of the tooth surfaces on drive and coast. You just need to increase the gear backlash to correct this pattern.

Break-In Procedure

The original equipment gears that came with your car or truck have a special phosphate coating on them. This coating offers additional protection to the gear tooth faces during the break-in mileage of the axle. Most aftermarket gears do not have this coating and therefore a break-in procedure is required.

Even with this coating, I highly recommend a break-in procedure for any rebuild and new gears. Keep in mind that the higher offset of the 9-inch axle makes it prone to more heat generation than the 8.8-inch axle. New gears and bearings tend to generate more heat until they are broken-in. Always use the gear manufacturer's recommendation for break-in procedure and lubrication.

The first 100 miles is the most critical. Use the axle at street speeds of 30 to 45 mph and stay below 60 mph for the first trip, which is usually less than 15 miles. Then allow the axle to cool for at least 30 minutes. Repeat this process for the first 100 miles on the new gears. Never subject the axle to full throttle or aggressive throttle accelerations in the first 500 miles because this exposes the components to excessive heat and can cause premature failure. Also never go to the race track within the first 500 miles because the axle is not prepared to withstand extreme loads.

During the break-in procedure, force speed differences across the clutch pack by driving in circles (clockwise and counterclockwise or figure 8s) to move lube through the clutch pack.

Change the axle oil after the first 500 miles. This removes any metal debris that was generated during break-in and if the oil was partially overheated, it is replaced. This may be a little too cautious, but the cost of oil is cheap insurance to make certain that you have years of hassle-free performance.

Gear Ratio Selection and Tooth Combinations

As modern vehicles have become more refined and quiet, a certain level of gear design and attention to gear tooth mesh frequency is required. The pinion is usually the weaker gear in the gear train and the more teeth on the pinion the better. The OE gears typically avoid having pinions with fewer than nine teeth on them. It is possible to make smaller pinions work but they may require special grades of steel and heat-treat processes.

Non-Hunting Ratio

The Ford 9-inch axle came from the factory with ratios that are whole numbers, such as 3.0:1, which was achieved with a 39-tooth ring gear meshing with a 13-tooth pinion gear.

This type of ratio is referred to as non-hunting because any given pinion tooth always contacts the same three-ring gear teeth per revolution.

An easy way to tell if you have a non-hunting ratio is to find out whether there is a whole number that can be multiplied by your ratio to come up with a whole-number result. For example, a 3.55:1 ratio cannot be multiplied by any whole number to get a whole number, so it is not non-hunting. But a 3.50:1 ratio can be multiplied by many whole numbers to get a whole number (2 for example, yielding another whole number, 7.0), so it is non-hunting.

The other way to tell is to write down the two multiplication pairs of each tooth-count and look for common factors. For instance 13 is a prime number, which has no whole number multiplication pairs, but 39 is not a prime number and has the factors 3 and 13. If there are no common factors, it is a non-hunting gear.

Typically, a non-hunting ratio is timed, meaning it has timing marks on the ring and pinion teeth that need

Following the break-in procedure and using the correct lubricant is crucial. This gear set was assembled and immediately driven to the track. The axle was filled with high-quality synthetic oil in the hope that it would allow the break-in process to be skipped. There was so much heat generated that the pinion teeth literally melted and tore off the shaft. Again, it is not recommended to use synthetic oil during break-in, especially on 9-inch gears.

Ring and Pinion Tooth Combinations

Ratio (:1)	Ring Teeth	Pinion Teeth	Common Factor	Ratio (:1)	Ring Teeth	Pinion Teeth	Common Factor
2.73	41	15	none	3.82	42	11	none
2.80	42	15	none	3.89	35	9	none
2.86	40	14	2	4.00	36	9	3
2.91	32	11	none	4.10	41	10	none
3.00	39	13	3	4.11	37	9	none
3.07	43	14	none	4.22	38	9	none
3.08	40	13	none	4.30	43	10	none
3.10	31	10	none	4.33	39	9	3
3.15	41	13	none	4.44	40	9	none
3.25	39	12	3	4.50	36	8	2, 4
3.27	36	11	none	4.56	41	9	none
3.31	43	13	none	4.63	37	8	none
3.33	40	12	2, 4	4.71	33	7	none
3.45	38	11	none	4.86	34	7	none
3.50	35	10	5	5.00	30	6	2, 3
3.55	39	11	none	5.14	36	7	none
3.60	36	10	2	5.50	33	6	3
3.70	37	10	none	5.67	34	6	2
3.73	41	11	none	5.83	35	6	none
3.75	45	12	3	6.00	30	5	5

This is a list of some common ratios and their gear and pinion tooth combinations. The 8.8-inch factory and service ratios are highlighted in yellow. The 9-inch ratios from the factory are in blue. The ratio 4.56:1 (in green) is common for both axle sizes.

You can see how the 2.86, 3.00, 3.25, 3.50:1, etc. are prone to gear whine issues, simply based on tooth combination. So, depending on the need for a specific ratio, I avoid the tooth combinations that are prone to make noise, which are the ratios with a common factor. This is not to say that all non-hunting ratios are noisy but if the vehicle is sensitive to this type of frequency, these ratios cause a problem. Ironically, many aftermarket gears with a 3.70:1 ratio tend to make noise.

Note that the list only includes ratios up to 6.0:1. There are even higher values available in the aftermarket.

to be aligned during assembly. The main reason for this is to re-match the teeth to each other that were matched during the lapping process when the gears were produced. If the marks are not aligned correctly, there is usually a gear whine issue in the vehicle and the contact pattern may be less than ideal. If you have an OE whole-number ratio, look for these timing marks. Aftermarket gears typically do not have them.

Semi-Hunting Ratio

A semi-hunting gear ratio is a ratio that has common factors, but the number of revolutions for them to come in contact again is more than a single revolution. A 3.5:1 ratio is a good example because it has a tooth combination of 35 and 10. A common factor of 5 is the tooth combination, but because the pinion with 10 teeth is not a prime number, it requires more than one ring gear revolution to align with the same pinion tooth. In this case, two revolutions are required in order for the pinion and ring teeth to align as they started. This type of ratio should also have timing marks but do not always come this way.

Full-Hunting Ratio

A full hunting (or just hunting) tooth combination is desirable for its low noise along with ease of lapping. This is the reason that most modern ratios utilize prime numbers for the tooth combinations. In other words, the pinion teeth mesh with most of the ring gear prior to encountering the original tooth.

PERFORMANCE 9-INCH AXLE INSTALLATION

One primary reason to rebuild a Ford 9-inch axle is to go along with a total performance drivetrain upgrade in your muscle car. One of the most common reasons to replace a wimpy stock axle assembly is that it could only handle the torque from the stock engine. But after you built or swapped in a high-performance engine, the output far exceeds the strength of the rear axle assembly.

Whether you have a Chevelle, Barracuda, Camaro, or Mustang there are aftermarket companies that sell these axles, ready to bolt-in for common applications. Currie Enterprises, Moser Engineering, and Strange Engineering are just a few of them.

A 1957 Chevy Bel Air makes a good project car. The Tri-Five Chevys are unique, highly sought after, and often upgraded. In addition to the powertrain upgrade detailed in this chapter, other upgrades typically performed include installing a Chevy 454-ci big-block engine, Tremec Magnum 6-speed transmission, McLeod clutch system, and of course the custom 9-inch axle. Also common is to add a tubular front suspension with revised steering geometry, power disc brakes at all four corners, and new wheels and tires.

Vehicle Acquisition and Inspection

The fine art of the deal is the first step in any new project, unless, of course, you already have a project vehicle in hand.

I have been scouting quite a few cars from a gentleman in the Detroit area for almost five years. We were finally able to come to an

This car was extracted from the back of the heated barn in the background. I already rinsed off years of dirt and debris. In 1972, the car had been returned to its original paint color, Adobe Beige. And then it was immediately sold and put in this barn. The trim was never re-installed and even some of the masking tape is still on the headlights. When it was packed into the barn in 1972, it was a running car but not any longer. The windshield was replaced and still has the installer's decal on it, which is interesting as the glass has already started delaminating and never saw even one road mile.

agreement for one of his Tri-Fives. So on a beautiful fall day, I loaded up the trailer and with the help of a friend, we went to retrieve this classic. It was truly an adventure as what was supposed to be a simple hour-long task of loading the car turned into a half-day's worth of

work to move all of the other classic cars out of the way.

With the project car finally in the shop, I began assessing what stays and what gets replaced and upgraded. Unfortunately, moisture was trapped in the carpet of the car and the outer perimeter of the floor

and floor braces are rusted through and need to be replaced. The powertrain is not numbers matching and I feel that a big-block upgrade done correctly will not detract from the value of the car. (Of course, the purist out there probably disagrees with me.) Building a car that is powerful

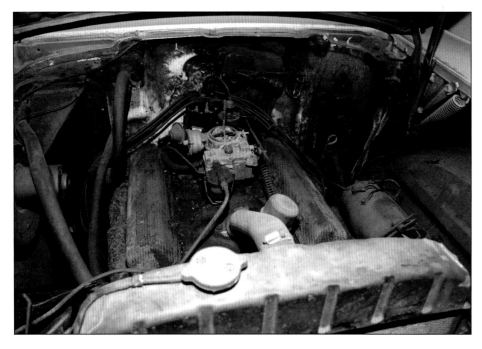

This Chevy 283-ci small-block is out of a Chevelle with an iron Powerglide transmission. I was not sure if this was a running car as the plug wires and part of the wiring were no longer connected and most of the transmission linkage had never been connected. But none of this really matters as I am going to replace all of this with a Chevy big-block and modern Tremec 6-speed transmission. The firewall shows traces of the previous metallic blue and the original Adobe Beige color.

When I brought the car home, it was a big day at the Palazzolo house. You can see the delaminated windshield and missing trim pieces. Also, you may recognize one of my helpers from my first book. This is one of my twin boys, Adrian, and he is eager to help out with a new project. I am going to need his help along with his brother's, Christian, to get this old classic back on the road.

The car sits very low in the back. Not only is it tucking the tires, but it is tucking a decent portion of the rear wheel up in the wheel well. As it turns out, a previous owner decided to lower the rear end with a torch on the leaf springs. This is a perfect example of how not to lower a car. You can also see the home-fabricated trailer hitch, definitely not appropriate for pulling a boat.

The clutch is one of the key elements for driveability. One of the biggest challenges of transferring 700 hp through a manual transmission is the clutch. Fortunately, McLeod Racing makes a twin-disc street clutch along with a hydraulic actuation system that's perfect for this engine and car. Here you can see the billet flywheel, twin disc clutch, and scattershield plate in place on the back of the engine. These parts are built for show and go. It is amazing how beautiful they are right out of the box and how well they perform in the car.

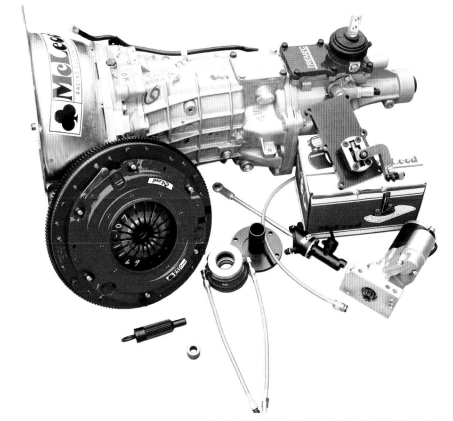

An awesome twin-disc clutch is installed behind the McLeod Racing bellhousing and the Tremec T56 Magnum 6-speed transmission. This transmission was originally set up for the newer LS-style engines, but the aftermarket McLeod bellhousing takes care of the interface to the big-block. McLeod produces all of the hydraulic actuation pieces, high-torque starter, and a custom shifter for the 1957 Bel Air. I recommend you always replace the pilot bearing while the system is apart.

yet driveable is the plan. This means modern power disc brakes at all four corners, power steering, and air conditioning to complement the drivetrain upgrades.

Drivetrain Upgrades

I have decided to put together a drivetrain that can withstand 700 hp, be easy to drive, and be reliable. This was a virtually impossible (or very expensive) task 15 years ago but with the current status of the aftermarket industry, it is now very achievable. The easiest way to get large horsepower numbers is through the use of a large-displacement engine. I am starting with the old-school Chevrolet 454 big-block.

Transmission Installation

The Tremec T-56 Magnum is rated at 700 ft-lbs of torque at the input shaft and is truly a brute of a gearbox. This transmission is an aftermarket version of the Tremec TR-6060 unit that is used in many of today's most hard-hitting sports cars,

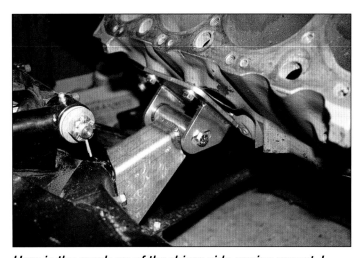

Here is the mock-up of the driver-side engine mount. I eliminated the stock-style front and rear engine mount arrangement and substituted a modern-style mid-block mount and transmission crossmember. These parts from Williams Classic Chassis Works are beautiful works of art and allow for better header and exhaust clearance. Note that the mount is slotted to allow for some adjustability to help clear aftermarket power-steering conversions. These mounts can be arranged for a stock rear block face position and a 3/4-inch forward position for additional firewall clearance to accommodate HEI distributors.

The complete engine, transmission, lowered front suspension with Hellwig sway bar, and exhaust are in place in the chassis. Again, the Williams Classis Chassis transmission crossmember and headers are a perfect fit and look awesome. The engine and transmission mounts have been welded in place. The transmission tips down at about 4 degrees (most engines are in the 3- to 5-degree range). Carbureted-style intake manifolds even take this into consideration, and these are wedge shaped so the carburetor is level in the vehicle. The pinion points up, toward the engine, at about 3 degrees.

meaning that it is not only strong but that it will easily deliver years of reliable performance and super smooth shift performance. This level of refinement cannot be found in any other manual transmission available in the aftermarket, making it a great upgrade, rather than reworking 1960s Muncie technology.

There are two ratio sets available and I chose the arrangement with the following ratios (first to sixth): 2.66, 1.78, 1.30, 1.0, 0.80, and 0.63:1 rather than a 2.97 first with a .74/.50 double overdrive. This offers the best of all worlds with a reasonably steep first gear and two overdrives that help to reduce the big-block's fuel consumption, without going too tall on the overdrive. If the overdrive is too tall, then the engine could lug, which means that the engine RPM is too low at highway or cruising speeds.

The Magnum transmission coupled to a 4.11:1 axle ratio with 28-inch-tall tires makes a very streetable combination, offering economy, strength, and durability. For this particular custom car build, a 4.11:1 works best for this combination. Many just assume a 4.11 is what they need, but that is not always the case. The section "Axle Ratio Selection" (page 142) includes information to help you select the correct gear ratio for your application. There are many cars with 4.11s running at much higher RPM just screaming at highway speeds. This is not what you necessarily want for a street car.

The Magnum's claim to fame is offering all of the quality and refinement of a modern original-equipment transmission in a package that is ideally suited for muscle car and hot rod builds.

The T-56 Magnum is basically a TR-6060 transmission in an aftermarket wrapper. Instead of using an integral bellhousing, it uses a T-56-style mid-plate that allows for adaptation to a variety of engines because the aftermarket offers a wide selection of bellhousings. Additionally, while minor sheet-metal modifications to the floor tunnel may be required due to its size, multiple shift locations and dual speedometer pickups allow for many different configurations.

The TR-6060 is found on the Dodge Challenger SRT-8, Viper SRT-10, C6 Corvette, Camaro SS and ZL1, Cadillac CTS-v, and Mustang Shelby GT500. All of these applications use the same basic transmission with minor variations. The transmission can easily support sustained input torque of 700 ft-lbs and shifts near the 8,000-rpm range.

Tremec has a network of "Elite Distributors" that offer many swap support parts such as cables, adaptors, clutches, release components, and transmission crossmembers for most popular applications.

The flexibility features of the Magnum are lessons learned and applied from the TKO 5-speed transmissions that most of us are familiar with. The main differences between the TKO and the Magnum are that the Magnum is a modern "end-loader" style of transmission and the older TKO is a "Toploader" style. The Magnum also features a great deal more refinement, strength, and high-RPM shifting capabilities. The Magnum overdrive gears, specifically fifth and sixth gears, are completely interchangeable. So it can be configured with the 2.97:1 first gears for low-end grunt and could use either the .74/.50 or .80/.63 double-overdrive gear ratios. However, care needs to be taken with an axle ratio that is too high numerically as the propshaft speed may possibly be too fast for a standard propshaft.

Spring Pocket Kit Installation

The entire reason for putting this powertrain together is to match the needs of a well-built Ford 9-inch axle. It does not make sense to have a bulletproof axle with no real power going through it. Let's face it: You purchased this book and probably a 9-inch axle because the stock unit is just too weak for all the horsepower your new engine produces. Therefore, it doesn't make sense to put this all together and try to put the power to the pavement through skinny little tires.

I wanted to tuck in some 13-inch-wide tires and still have the car 2 inches lower than stock all the way around. The only way to achieve that is by installing a spring pocket kit.

1 Inspect Components

Here are the pieces that come in the Williams Classic Chassis Works spring pocket kit. The plan is to move the leaf springs, which are mounted outside the frame rails, into pockets that move them under the frame rails while still maintaining the correct spring mounting heights. The pockets and reinforcement brackets are a little long and require some trimming to fit perfectly. This universal kit works with both one- and two-piece frames, and that is why some minor trimming is required.

2 Remove Springs and Axle

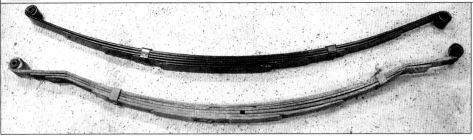

Remove the old springs and axle (see Chapter 2 for more details). Often the fasteners are rusty, which makes this difficult. The original leaf spring sits next to an aftermarket 2-inch-lowered spring. Notice the rear eyelet (at the right) is reversed to achieve the required drop. Also, on this original spring (bottom) the sharp bend of about 4 inches from either end was handled with a torch and basically ruined the springs. You can see that even the center spring is cracked in half and separating from the pack. The old springs are junk at this stage.

3 Mark Perch Alignment

Precision Measurement

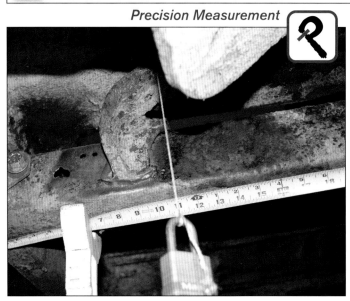

Take measurements and mark where the stock leaf spring perches align with the frame rail for the installation of the spring pocket kit. You can use a homemade plumb bob to measure and mark the location of the rear spring hanger pivot. The marks and measurements serve as a reference point for notching the frame rail later.

This is one of the front spring perches, which needs to be removed from the frame. I have marked the spot welds and arc welds with white chalk, so you can see the welds that need to be drilled and ground off. This is a two-piece frame and the body has been taken off the frame; the frame has been flipped upside down.

4 Remove Perch Rivets

The rear perch was riveted to the side of the frame and a weld was placed along the top. (Don't forget that the frame is upside down in this photo.) I have marked the two rivets with white chalk (left). You just grind the heads off with an angle grinder and punch the rivets through (right). You could also drill the rivets out of the brackets.

If you have a one-piece frame, you need to temporarily clamp the front spring pocket next to the frame to make some marks to guide the cutting for fitting the pocket in place.

5 Align Front Perches

You can use a 1/2-inch piece of threaded rod through the entire frame to help align the front perches. Here you see the area that needs to be removed (outlined in yellow). The grind marks are from the welds that you removed from the original front spring bracket. Cut just inside the yellow and slowly open up the hole to get the pocket to fit perfectly.

For reference, on two-piece frames, the rectangular hole needs to be as wide as the bottom of the frame. On one-piece frames, the width of the rectangle is narrow, so be careful not to cut the hole too large.

6 Cut Front Pocket Hole

This hole was cut in the one-piece frame. Do not cut the entire bottom surface of the frame all the way to the side of the frame rail. Leave a small portion of the bottom surface in place. If you find mouse carcasses or old nests, as I did in this car, just vacuum them out.

7 Weld In Front Pockets

A single-piece frame with the front pockets in place is ready for welding. One of the pockets has been welded in place on a two-piece frame. On the two-piece frame, I have added a rear shock crossmember (from Williams Classis Chassis Works). This way the frame has more rigidity and the shock loads go into the frame and not into the floor or the trunk.

I recommend that an experienced professional perform this "upside down" welding because falling weld spatter is very dangerous. If you are going to do it, here are a couple of items to keep in mind: Use the same heat settings as if you were welding right side up and keep the amount of wire "stick out" as short as possible (within 3/8 inch). The short stick out transfers more heat to the welder tip, so take your time and let the tip cool. Stitch these pockets in to avoid adding too much heat to any single area.

8 Align Rear Perches

For the rear spring perch, the yellow line on the frame matches your earlier marks from the stock location and your measurements. Clamp the new bracket on the top of the frame (remember, it is upside down) with the center of the hole aligned with the yellow line.

Use the measurements from the instructions (from the rear of the frame rail along the filler piece) as a template to mark the area that needs to be cut out of the frame.

The vertical lines represent the centerline of the spring perch and the rearward edge, where the slant begins. Start with the spring perch center, then the start of the angled portion, carry that angle to the bottom of the frame, and use the filler piece as a template. I recommend marking the frame about 1/4 inch short so you can slowly fine-tune the notch with an angle grinder for a perfect fit.

9 Cut Rear Pocket Hole

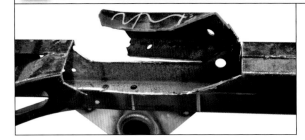

Here is the rough cut-out portion. You just need to finish grinding with an angle grinder and metal prep the notch to get it perfect.

10 Weld In Frame Notch Filler

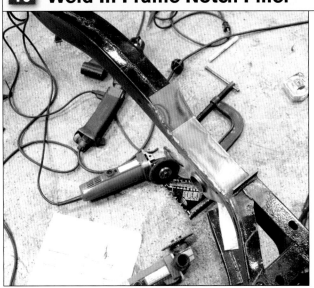

It is paramount to have clean steel surfaces that are free of any rust, paint, or oil prior to welding. All of these things contaminate the weld and compromise the strength. I suggest practicing welder settings on a scrap piece to avoid any mistakes on the real parts.

Use a MIG welder to attach the frame notch filler piece on the bottom of the frame rail. (The length of the notch piece accommodates both styles of frames.) It's best to alternate the weld pattern from side to side and front to back (called stitching) while allowing time for the steel to cool. This helps to avoid any distortion from the heat. The filler piece still needs to be trimmed and metal finished. Then repeat for the other side.

You can also refer to the sketch that comes with the kit instructions for the notch geometry and location of the bracket on top of the frame.

11 Weld In Perch Brackets

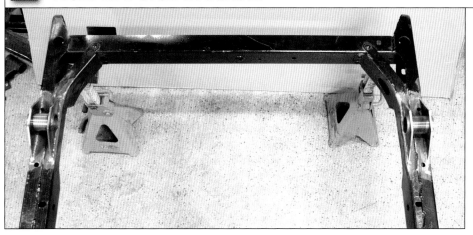

You can now solidly weld in the perch brackets. If these brackets are welded in place with the body still on the frame, which is possible, you do not have complete access along the length of the brackets. In that situation, you need to fabricate a little rectangular piece to cap off the angle ends of the brackets to provide more support and structure.

The new spring arrangement has the spring shackles straddle the frame rail.

Here is a close-up picture of the bracket on top of the frame and notch below the frame. This is much easier to weld in place with the body off the vehicle but it is still possible with the body on. If the body is left on and you cannot get full welds along the plates, you can add filler plates on the angled surfaces that can be welded across the frame for further support.

12 Weld Traction Bars to Frame

While the frame is still upside down weld the brackets for the traction bars to the frame and fit them inside the front portion of the spring pocket plates.

Shown here, the leaf spring is in place and the traction bar is just roughly assembled. (Of course, for the final assembly, the axle is installed.) Note that the traction bar is backward, as the threaded adjustment portion should be on the frame side and not the spring side.

Traction bars stop the front portion of the leaf spring from winding up during hard launches. This also limits the pinion rotation upward during launches. It is a common misconception that the pinion should be oriented downward so that during hard accelerations, the axle housing rotates upward and the driveline angles all line up. This may be fine for some leaf spring vehicles but it is more often than not incorrect. The pinion should be oriented to be parallel with the transmission angle at ride height. Ideally you want the working angle across each joint to be in the 1- to 3-degree range with a difference from each of about 1/2 degree. This car is set up with the engine down 4 degrees and the axle is built with the pinion up 3 degrees.

Wheel Tub Installation

The spring pocket kit installation moves the springs underneath the frame rails and allows for wider than factory rear wheels and tires. Typically you can get an 8-inch-wide tire in place. The real benefit is when you also mini-tub the car. This allows at least a 13-inch-wide tire; some have even squeezed in a 13½-inch-wide tire without clear-ance problems. In my opinion, the spring pocket kit goes hand in hand with mini-tubs to get the most space for wide tires.

Many different methods can be used. I review using the old wheel tubs and adding a spacer, but using aftermarket wheel tubs can also achieve this. I prefer the look of the factory tub compared to the sharp corners of aftermarket tubs.

Also, to allow for exhaust clear-ance, I remove the spare tire well from the trunk and use a gas-tank centering bracket kit. This allows me to run the tailpipes inboard of the frame rails; they exit straight out the back of the car. Note that the spare-tire patch panel and gas-tank center-ing bracket kit came from Williams Classic Chassis Works.

1 Measure Trunk Area

This trunk is in its stock configuration. The wheel tubs are about 46½ inches apart. The spare tire well and jack brackets are still in place and the original factory-applied seam sealer is intact. (I have removed a portion of it just behind the jack mount by the spare tire well.)

Cut the wheel tubs at the top of the arch for each tub in a straight line from front to back. Then weld in about a 3-inch-wide steel strip to space the tubs inboard, so the vertical surface of the wheel well matches the frame rail.

2 Spot Weld Steel Support

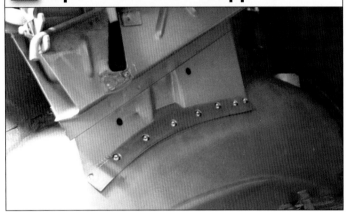

Remove the trunk lid to allow for room while working and to remove the weight from the hinge supports. There is a steel support that is spot welded to the wheel tubs on both sides. Drill out the spot welds and cut the bracket where it meets the trunk hinge support. Save these brackets and just re-weld them to the same location on the wheel tub after it is moved inboard. Butt weld the top portion to the inboard side of the hinge bracket.

3 Mark Cut Lines

Behind the rear seat there is a support structure for the rear of the car. You need to cut it loose and trim it so you can slide the tub inboard.

Make a chalk line as a rough mark of the cuts you need to make. Fold the U-shaped portion at the top up and temporarily out of the way. Once the tub is in its new location, you can bend this flap back down and weld it back into place.

4 Cut Out Driver-Side Wheel Tub

Remove the driver-side wheel tub and trunk hinge support. Also remove the seam sealer and mark a line for cutting. (The support behind the back seat has already been trimmed.)

You can use a flexible magnetic strip and straight edge to lay out the cut line prior to marking. This cut line needs to be straight so the filler piece is easier to install without gaps to fill.

The bulge at the back of the driver-side tub is where it meets the trunk floor. This is for the gas tank filler tube and the reason the marked line has a slight jog in it. (A small, rectanglular filler piece will be added later.)

For this side, I cut about 2 inches away from the seam; notice the black line. Once the tub has been removed, trim the underside where the tub meets the trunk floor (this is required or else the flange below the floor interferes with the frame rail) and re-weld the pieces together. This then allows you to slide the tub over and then butt weld it.

4 Cut Out Driver-Side Wheel Tub CONTINUED

The driver's side tub has been removed and some of the surrounding steel has been cleaned for welding. The floor still needs to be trimmed to allow for the new tub to slide in place. After further inspection, I discovered that the inner wheel well had rusted through previously. Instead of cutting and patching the hole, someone pushed in body filler and nothing is supporting it. These areas will be patched correctly with the final prep of the trunk. You can also see the undercoating in the inner fender well area. The undersides of the tubs were similarly covered. I removed this with the help of some carefully applied heat and a copper scraper.

5 Cut Out Passenger-Side Wheel Tub

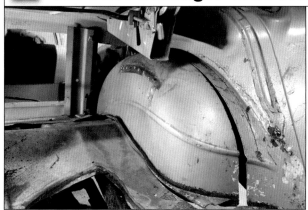

Perform the same process for the passenger's side, except you do not need to jog the cut for the filler tube bulge. Here, the tub has been cut out but it is still in place. You also need to cut out the spare tire well and patch it with a panel.

6 Inspect Cuts

The passenger-side inner wheel well and trunk floor is shown. The hole at the top of the picture is from the missing wheel tub and the hole just beyond the frame rail is from the spare tire well. You can also see how severe the kink was torched in the stock leaf spring.

7 Remove Back Seat Support

After you remove the spare tire well and both wheel tubs, remove the remainder of the back seat support structure. To gain more working space to get grinders and welders in place, you may want to remove the 40 or so spot welds and the bracing.

8 Inspect Spare Tire Well and Wheel Tub Spacers

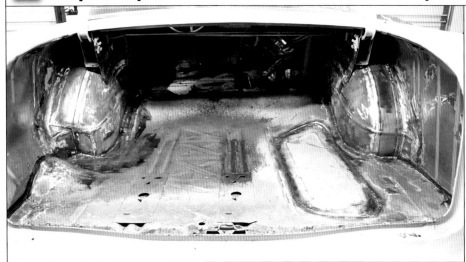

This is the roughed-in trunk with the spare tire well block-off plate and the wheel tub spacers in place. There is still a fair amount of metal preparation required before you paint.

9 Prep Frame for Mounting Shocks

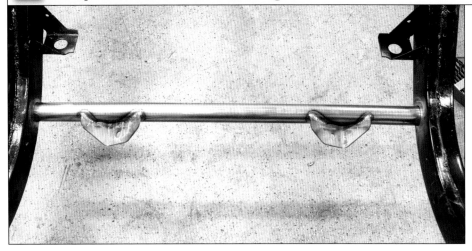

On page 123, Step 7, I showed the new rear shock crossmember already welded in place. This was pretty straightforward and the crossmember comes with good directions for the measurements. Now you need to use a hole saw to drill a couple of holes in the frame to allow the tube to fit inside, prep the area for welding, and align the tube correctly.

On the left is an undamaged leaf spring plate with the factory shock stud in place, and on the right is the modified plate. The new rear shocks came with studs for replacement. I modified the stud, which is the stud in the foreground, to have a 1/2-inch-diameter shoulder that fits into the 1/2-inch hole that I drilled in the bracket. I left a .100-inch-thick shoulder to simulate the stock stud. I just press the modified stud in the bracket; plug weld the back side solid, and weld the spacer portion as well. After primer and paint, it will look just like the original.

Axle Ratio Selection

After choosing the wheels and tires, I need to take measurements for the custom 9-inch axle. I was conservative on the tire width and wanted to balance the gap between the wheel well and frame rail. In order to center everything, I ended up having the axle fabricated to a rotor mounting face overall width of 54 inches.

Keep in mind that it is very convenient nowadays to purchase a crate engine and a transmission built to handle tons of power. Why wouldn't you buy a crate rear end to complete the drivetrain? Most people forget about the axle assembly and try to get a stock or poorly rebuilt unit to work. Of course, the result is a disaster when the axle fails.

There are several ways to select an axle ratio. For all-out drag racing, you want to calculate shift points, so the car runs through the end of the track traps at maximum power while avoiding time wasted with unnecessary shifts.

I am building a fun street car and want to have a car that is not running at crazy high engine speeds while on the highway. I want about 2,000 rpm at 65 mph. So, the basic formula is:

$$\text{Engine Speed} = (\text{vehicle speed} \times \text{axle ratio} \times \text{transmission ratio} \times 336) \div \text{tire diameter}.$$

For my target car the numbers go like this:

$$(65 \times 4.11 \times 0.63 \times 336) \div 28$$
$$2{,}019 \text{ rpm}$$

For a traditional 454 engine, this is probably the lowest that I want to be on the torque curve and still easily pass someone on the highway. Of course, if I really want to pass aggressively, I can downshift to fifth or even fourth gear. This is another benefit of the Tremec 6-speed transmission.

On the other end, the 2.66 first gear combined with the 4.11:1 axle ratio yields tons of torque in first gear to get the car moving in a hurry. What really makes this combination work is the large-diameter tires, 4.11:1 axle ratio, and the flexibility of 6-speed ratios.

The custom rear axle from Currie Enterprises was built with a custom-polished center section. It features the large Torino-style tapered wheel bearings, 11-inch Explorer disc brakes, a nodular-iron third member stuffed with 4.11:1 gears, and the clutch-plate-style Traction-Lok, 31-tooth limited-slip differential. It even has the larger Daytona-style pinion support cartridge and bearings. The leaf spring pads are already welded in place for the pinion to point upward at 3 degrees and a spacing of 38¾ inches to match the new leaf spring location. It also has an upgraded 1350-style universal joint flange. This axle assembly is all set for handling 700 hp. It is really hard to beat this type of setup.

Note that the area over the axle has a lot of hardware: shocks, exhaust, and Hellwig sway bar, but it all fits perfectly. As you can see, the exhaust is only tied in place for now. I will fix this once I finish the engine break-in. The last thing to do to complete the back half of the car is to route the hydraulic brake lines and the parking brake cables.

You can see the spring pocket kit and the 2-inch lowered springs are supporting the frame. The traction bars are in place to handle hard launches. The Currie 11-inch discs provide ample stopping power. Of course, I can't forget to mention the whole reason for most of these changes is to accommodate the 13-inch-wide rear tires.

Summary

Installing a 9-inch axle is a great performance upgrade for any hot rod or muscle car. If you are setting up a new project car or have outgrown the stock axle, a Ford 9-inch axle is a great way to go. With the advent of aftermarket support, it is easy to put together an axle for just about any vehicle, as shown with the Currie unit in this 1957 Bel Air.

Of course, the axle is a very important and often overlooked part of the drivetrain upgrade process. The axle, and more specifically axle ratio, and tire size really tie together the entire powertrain along with the correct transmission ratios to give the best performance for the vehicle.

Do not fall into the old trap of just tossing a 4.11:1 axle ratio in your car and think that it will work just right. It just happened to be the ratio for this build, but don't forget the importance of tire size and transmission ratios.

While it seems that I have the perfect plan and build, a project always presents a challenge or two to overcome. So plan on being surprised at some point during the build. Granted the weight of the body is not on the chassis, but the initial setup had the axle pinion pointing down by 1 degree. After many different measurements, I determined that the lowering springs were the cause of the problem. This was not supposed to happen but something went wrong when the springs were produced. This is a real shame because these springs lower the car and move the axle rearward to help center the tires in wheel wells. For the sake of moving forward with the project, I purchased a couple different sets of pinion shims. This is a picture of the aluminum 2½ degree shims that I didn't use. I ended up with a set of 4-degree cast-iron shims to correct the pinion angle. I highly recommend using cast-iron shims, which are readily available from most speed shops for about $20 per set.

The other option is to cut off the spring perches, re-orient the axle, and weld them back in place. I chose the angled shim route as the axle was already assembled and painted and this also gives me some flexibility if I need to tweak the shim later. I did preload the suspension, front and rear, to take the measurements and build confidence that the 4-degree shim was the correct way to go.

9-Inch Axle Identification Codes

Code	Application/Year	Ratio (:1)	Ring Gear Diam (inches)	Diff Type	Axle Shaft Splines	Code	Application/Year	Ratio (:1)	Ring Gear Diam (inches)	Diff Type	Axle Shaft Splines
S704B	E150 '81–87	3.00	9.00	open	28	WBT-BC	Ford Pass. Car	3.50	8.75	open	
S705B	E150 '81–87	3.00	9.00	l-slip	31	WBT-BD	Ford Pass. Car	3.89	8.75	open	
S714A	E150 '81–87	3.50	9.00	open	28	WBT-BE	Ford Pass. Car	3.25	9.00	open	
S715A	E150 '81–87	3.50	9.00	l-slip	31	WBT-BG	Ford Pass. Car	3.89	9.00	open	
S716P	E150 '81–87	3.50	9.00	open	28	WBT-BM	Pass. Car '63–64	3.50	8.75	open*	
S716S	E150 '81–87	3.50	9.00	open	28	WBT-BN	Ford Pass. Car	3.50	8.75	open	
S717P	E150 '81–87	3.50	9.00	l-slip	31	WBT-BP	Pass. Car '63–64	3.25	8.75	open*	
S717S	E150 '81–87	3.50	9.00	l-slip	31	WBT-BR	Ford Pass. Car	3.25	8.75	open	
WBG-E	F100 '63–72	3.70	9.00	open	28	WBT-BS	Ford Pass. Car	3.00	8.75	open	
WBG-F	F100 '63–72	3.89	9.00	open	28	WBT-BT	Pass. Car '64	3.00	8.75	open*	
WBG-H	F100 '63–72	3.89	9.00	open	28	WBT-BU	Pass. Car '63–64	3.00	9.00	open	
WBG-L	F100 '63–72	4.11	9.00	open	28	WBT-BV	Pass. Car '63–64	3.00	9.00	open	
WBS-AD	Pass. Car '63–64	3.00	8.75	open		WBT-BY	Pass. Car '63–64	3.50	9.00	open*†	
WBS-AE	Pass. Car '63–64	3.50	8.75	open		WBT-BZ	Pass. Car '63–64	3.89	9.00	open*†	
WBS-AG	Ford Pass. Car	3.00	9.00	open		WBT-CA	Pass. Car '63–64	4.11	9.00	open*†	
WBS-AK	Ford Pass. Car	3.00	8.75	open		WBT-CB	Pass. Car '63–64	3.25	8.75	open*	
WBS-AL	Ford Pass. Car	3.50	8.75	open		WBT-CD	Pass. Car '64	3.89	8.75	open*	
WBS-AP	Ford Pass. Car	3.89	8.75	open		WBT-CE	Pass. Car '64	3.00	8.75	open	
WBS-AR	Ford Pass. Car '63	3.25	8.75	open		WBT-CF	Pass. Car '64	3.25	8.75	open	
WBS-AS	Ford Pass. Car	3.25	8.75	open		WBT-CG	Pass. Car '64	3.50	8.75	open	
WBS-AT	Ford Pass. Car	3.25	9.00	open		WBT-CK	Pass. Car '64	3.25	9.00	open	
WBS-AU	Ford Pass. Car	3.50	9.00	open		WBT-CL	Pass. Car '64	3.50	9.00	open	
WBS-AV	Pass. Car '63–64	3.89	8.75	open*		WBT-N	Pass. Car '63	3.89	8.75	open	
WBS-AY	Pass. Car '63–64	3.50	8.75	open*		WBT-W	Pass. Car '63–64	3.00	8.75	open	
WBS-AZ	Ford Pass. Car	3.50	9.00	open		WBT-X	Pass. Car '63–64	3.50	8.75	open	
WBS-BA	Ford Pass. Car	3.89	9.00	open		WBT-Y	Pass. Car	3.50	8.75	open	
WBS-BB	Ford Pass. Car	3.50	8.75	open		WBT-Z	Pass. Car	4.11	8.75	open	
WBS-BC	Ford Pass. Car	3.89	8.75	open		WBU-AA	Pass. Car	3.89	8.75	open	
WBS-BD	Ford Pass. Car	3.89	9.00	open		WBU-AB	Pass. Car	3.50	8.75	l-slip	
WBS-B	Pass. Car '63–64	3.00	8.75	open*		WBU-L	Pass. Car	3.89	8.75	l-slip	
WBS-BH	Pass. Car '63	3.25	8.75	open*		WBU-R	Pass. Car	3.00	8.75	l-slip	
WBS-BJ	Pass. Car '63	3.50	8.75	open*		WBU-S	Pass. Car	3.50	8.75	l-slip	
WBS-BL	Pass. Car '63–64	3.25	8.75	open*		WBU-T	Pass. Car	3.89	8.75	l-slip	
WBS-BN	Pass. Car '64	3.00	8.75	open		WBU-Z	Pass. Car	3.25	8.75	l-slip	
WBS-BR	Pass. Car '64	3.25	8.75	open		WBV-AA	Pass. Car '63	3.25	8.75	l-slip	
WBS-BU	Pass. Car '64	3.25	9.00	open		WBV-AB	Pass. Car '63–64	3.89	8.75	l-slip*	
WBS-K	Pass. Car '63	3.89	8.75	open		WBV-AC	Pass. Car '63–64	3.50	8.75	l-slip*	
WBT-AA	Pass. Car '63	3.00	9.00	open		WBV-AE	Pass. Car	3.25	9.00	l-slip	
WBT-AF	Ford Pass. Car	3.50	9.00	open		WBV-AF	Pass. Car	3.50	9.00	l-slip	
WBT-AG	Pass. Car '63	3.00	8.75	open		WBV-AG	Pass. Car	3.89	9.00	l-slip	
WBT-AH	Pass. Car '63	3.50	8.75	open		WBV-AH	Pass. Car	3.00	9.00	l-slip†	
WBT-AP	Pass. Car '63	3.89	8.75	Type		WBV-AJ	Pass. Car	3.50	9.00	l-slip†	
WBT-AR	Pass. Car '63–64	3.25	8.75	open		WBV-AK	Pass. Car	3.89	9.00	l-slip†	
WBT-AS	Pass. Car '63	3.25	8.75	open		WBV-AL	Pass. Car	4.11	9.00	l-slip†	
WBT-AT	Pass. Car '63–64	3.89	8.75	open*		WBV-AP	Pass. Car '63–64	3.50	8.75	l-slip*	
WBT-AU	Pass. Car '63–64	3.50	8.75	open*		WBV-AR	Pass. Car '63	3.25	8.75	l-slip*	
WBT-AV	Ford Pass. Car	3.00	9.00	open†		WBV-AS	Pass. Car '63–64	3.89	8.75	l-slip*	
WBT-AY	Ford Pass. Car	3.50	9.00	open†		WBV-AT	Pass. Car '64	3.00	8.75	l-slip*	
WBT-AZ	Ford Pass. Car	3.89	9.00	open†		WBV-AV	Pass. Car '63–64	3.00	9.00	l-slip	
WBT-BA	Ford Pass. Car	4.11	9.00	open†		WBV-AZ	Pass. Car '63	3.50	9.00	l-slip*†	
WBT-BB	Ford Pass. Car	3.50	9.00	open		WBV-BA	Pass. Car '63	3.89	9.00	l-slip*†	

* pinion damper style flange   ** 1/2-inch ring gear bolts   † 4-pinion   § high performance

Code	Application/Year	Ratio (:1)	Ring Gear Diam (inches)	Diff Type	Axle Shaft Splines
WBV-BB	Pass. Car '63	4.11	9.00	l-slip*†	
WBV-BC	Pass. Car '63	3.25	9.00	l-slip	
WBV-BD	Pass. Car '64	3.00	8.75	open	
WBV-BE	Pass. Car '64	3.50	8.75	l-slip	
WBV-BG	Pass. Car '64	3.50	9.00	l-slip	
WBV-H	Pass. Car '63	3.89	8.75	l-slip	
WBV-N	Pass. Car '63–64	3.00	8.75	l-slip	
WBV-P	Pass. Car '63–64	3.50	8.75	l-slip	
WCD-C	T-Bird '63–64	3.00	9.00	open	
WCD-D	T-Bird	3.00	9.00	open†	
WCD-E	T-Bird '65	3.00	9.00	open	28
WCD-F	T-Bird '65	3.50	9.00	open	28
WCD-G	T-Bird '65	3.25	9.00	open†	28
WCD-H	T-Bird '66	3.00	9.00	open	28
WCD-J	T-Bird '66	3.00	9.00	l-slip	28
WCN-A	Pass. Car '63	3.00	9.00	open**†	
WCN-B	Pass. Car '63–64	3.50	9.00	open**†	
WCN-C	Pass. Car '63–64	4.11	9.00	open**†	
WCN-D	Pass. Car '63	3.00	8.75	open	
WCN-E	Pass. Car '63–64	3.50	8.75	open	
WCN-G	Pass. Car '63	4.11	8.75	open	
WCN-H	Pass. Car '63	3.89	8.75	open	
WCN-J	Pass. Car '63	3.25	8.75	open	
WCN-K	Pass. Car '63–64	3.50	8.75	open*	
WCN-L	Pass. Car '63–64	3.89	8.75	open*	
WCN-M	Pass. Car '63	4.11	8.75	open*	
WCN-P	Pass. Car '63	3.50	8.75	open*	
WCN-R	Pass. Car '63	3.00	8.75	open*	
WCN-S	Pass. Car '63	3.25	8.75	open*	
WCN-U	Pass. Car '64	3.50	9.00	open*†	31
WCN-V	Pass. Car '64	4.11	9.00	open†	31
WCR-A	Van '63–67	4.11	9.00	open	28
WCR-B	Van '63–67	4.57	9.00	open	28
WCR-D	Van '63–67	3.50	9.00	open	28
WCR-E	Van '63–67	3.25	9.00	open	28
WCR-F	Van '63–67	3.00	9.00	open	28
WCR-G	Van '63–67	3.70	9.00	open	28
WCR-H	Van '63–67	4.11	9.00	open	28
WCR-J	Van '63–67	4.57	9.00	open	28
WCR-K	Van '63–67	3.50	9.00	open	28
WCR-L	Van '63–67	3.00	9.00	open	28
WCR-M	Van '63–67	4.11	9.00	open	28
WCR-N	Van '63–67	4.57	9.00	open	28
WCR-R	Van '63–67	3.50	9.00	open	28
WCR-S	Van '63–67	3.00	9.00	open	28
WCT-A	Pass. Car	3.00	9.00	l-slip†	
WCT-B	Pass. Car	3.50	9.00	l-slip†	
WCT-C	Pass. Car	4.11	9.00	l-slip†	
WCU-A	Fairlane '63–65	3.25	8.75	open	
WCU-B	Fairlane '63–65	3.50	8.75	open§	28
WCU-C	Fairlane '63–65	3.89	8.75	open§	28
WCU-D	Fairlane '63–65	4.11	8.75	open§	28
WCZ-H	Mustang '65	3.89	8.75	open§	28
WCZ-J	Mustang '65	4.11	8.75	open§	28
WCZ-P	Mustang '65	3.50	8.75	open§	28
WCZ-R	Mustang '66	3.50	8.75	open§	28
WCZ-S	Mustang '66	3.50	8.75	open§	28
WCZ-T	Mustang '66	3.50	8.75	l-slip§	28
WDC-A	Ford Pass. '65	3.00	8.75	open	28
	Ford Pass. '72 Mercury '72	2.75	9.00	open	28

Code	Application/Year	Ratio (:1)	Ring Gear Diam (inches)	Diff Type	Axle Shaft Splines
WDC-AA	Ford Pass. '65 Mercury '65	3.50	9.00	open	28
WDC-AB	Ford Pass. '65 Mercury '65	3.00	9.00	open*†	28
WDC-AC	Ford Pass. '65 Mercury '65	3.25	9.00	open*†	28
WDC-AD	Ford Pass. '65 Mercury '65	3.50	9.00	open*†	28
WDC-AE	Ford Pass. '65 Mercury '65	3.89	9.00	open*†	28
WDC-AF	Ford Pass. '65 Mercury '65	4.11	9.00	open*†	28
WDC-AG	Ford Pass. '65 Mercury '65	3.00	9.00	open	28
WDC-AK	Ford Pass. '65 Mercury '65	3.25	9.00	open	28
WDC-AL	Ford Pass. '65 Mercury '65	3.89	9.00	open	28
WDC-AM	Ford Pass. '65 Mercury '65	3.25	9.00	open	28
WDC-AN	Ford Pass. '65 Mercury '65	3.25	9.00	open*	28
WDC-AP	Ford Pass. '65	3.50	9.00	open*	28
WDC-AS	Ford Pass. '66–69	3.25			
WDC-AT	Ford Pass. '66–69 Mercury '66–67 T-Bird '67	3.00	9.00	open	28
WDC-AU	Ford Pass. '66–69 Mercury '66–69	3.25	9.00	open	28
WDC-AV	Ford Pass. '66–69	3.00	8.75	open	28
WDC-AVX	Forad Pass. '66	3.00	8.75	open	28
WDC-B	Ford Pass. '65	3.00	8.75	open	28
WDC-BS	Ford Pass. '66 Mercury '66	3.00	9.00	open	28
WDC-BT	Ford Pass. '66	3.00	9.00	open	28
WDC-BU	Ford Pass. '66	3.50	8.75	open	28
WDC-BY	Ford Pass. '66 Mercury '66	3.25	9.00	open	28
WDC-BZ	T-Bird '67	3.00	9.00	open	28
WDC-C	Ford Pass. '65	3.00			
WDC-CA	Ford Pass. '67–70	2.75	9.00	open	28
	Ford Pass. '72	3.00	9.00	open	28
	Mercury '67–70	2.75	9.00	open	28
	Mercury '72	3.00	9.00	open	28
WDC-CA4	Ford Pass. '67–73 Mercury '67–73	2.75	9.00	open	28
WDC-CA5	Ford Pass. '73 Mercury '75	2.75	9.00	open	28
WDC-CAX	Ford Pass. '67 Mercury '67	2.75	9.00	open	28
WDC-CB	Ford Pass. '67	3.00	8.75	open	28
WDC-CC	Ford Pass. '68–71 Mercury '68–71	3.00	9.00	open†	28
WDC-CE	Ford Pass. '68 Mercury '68	3.25	9.00	open	28
WDC-CF	Ford Pass. '68 Mercury '68	3.50	9.00	open	28
WDC-CG	Ford Pass. '68	3.00	8.75	open	28
WDC-CH	Ford Pass. '68	3.25	8.75	open	28
WDC-C	Ford Pass. '68 Mercury '68	2.75	9.00	open	28

* pinion damper style flange   ** 1/2-inch ring gear bolts   † 4-pinion   § high performance

Code	Application/Year	Ratio (:1)	Ring Gear Diam (inches)	Diff Type	Axle Shaft Splines	Code	Application/Year	Ratio (:1)	Ring Gear Diam (inches)	Diff Type	Axle Shaft Splines
WDC-CK	Ford Pass. '67–76 Mercury '67–76	3.25	9.00	open	28	WDC-EJ	Mercury '76	2.75	9.00	open†	28
WDC-CL	Ford Pass. '68–69 Mercury '68–69	3.25	9.00	open†	28	WDC-EK	Ford Pass. '77–78 Mercury '77–78	3.00	9.00	open	28
WDC-CM	Ford Pass. '68–69 Mercury '68–69	3.50	9.00	open†	28	WDC-EL	Ford Pass. '77	2.50	9.00	open	28
WDC-CN	Ford Pass. '69–71	2.75	9.00	open†	28		Ford Pass. '78, to 3/15/78	2.50	9.00	open	28
	Ford Pass. '74	3.25	9.00	open	28		Ford Pass. '78, from 3/15/78	2.47	9.00	open	28
	Mercury '69–71	2.75	9.00	open	28		Mercury '78, to 3/15/78	2.50	9.00	open	28
	Mercury '74	3.25	9.00	open	28		Mercury '78, from 3/15/78	2.47	9.00	open	28
WDC-CR	Ford Pass. '69–76 Mercury '69–76	3.25	9.00	open†	28	WDC-EM	Ford Pass. '77	2.50	9.00	open	28
WDC-CS	Ford Pass. '70–71	3.00	9.00	open	28		Ford Pass. '78, to 3/15/78	2.50	9.00	open	28
WDC-CU	Ford Pass. '73–76 Mercury '72–76	2.75					Ford Pass. '78, from 3/15/78	2.47	9.00	open	28
WDC-CV	Mercury '72	3.00	9.00	open†	28		Mercury '78, 2.50 to 3/15/78	2.50	9.00	open	28
WDC-CY	Mercury '73	2.75	9.00	open†	28		Mercury '78, from 3/15/78	2.47	9.00	open	28
WDC-CZ	Mercury '73–74	3.25	9.00	open†	28	WDC-F	Ford Pass. '65	3.50	8.75	open	28
WDC-D	Ford Pass. '65	3.25	8.75	open	28	WDC-FB	Ford Pass. '76 Mercury '76	3.25	9.00	open	28
WDC-DA	Ford Pass. '73–76 Mercury '73–76	3.00	9.00	open†	28	WDC-G	Ford Pass. '65	3.50	8.75	open*	28
WDC-DB	Mercury '73–76	2.75	9.00	open†	28	WDC-H	Ford Pass. '65	3.89	8.75	open	28
WDC-DD	Mercury '74	3.25	9.00	open†	28	WDC-J	Ford Pass. '65	3.89	8.75	open*	28
WDC-DF	Ford Pass. '73 Mercury '73	3.00	9.00	open	28	WDC-K	Ford Pass. '65 Mercury '65	3.00	9.00	open	28
WDC-DH	Ford Pass. '74–76 Mercury '74–76	2.75	9.00	open†	28	WDC-L	Ford Pass. '65	3.25	9.00	open*	28
WDC-DK	Mercury '74	2.75	9.00	open†	28	WDC-M	Ford Pass. '65 Mercury '65	3.50	9.00	open	28
WDC-DL	Mercury '74–76	3.25	9.00	open†	28	WDC-N	Ford Pass. '65	3.50	9.00	open*	28
WDC-DM	Ford Pass. '74 Mercury '74	3.00	9.00	open	28	WDC-P	Ford Pass. '65	3.89	9.00	open*	28
WDC-DN	Ford Pass. '74–76 Mercury '74–76	3.25	9.00	open	28	WDC-R	Ford Pass. '65	3.00	9.00	open†	28
WDC-DR	Ford Pass. '74–76 Mercury '74–76	3.00	9.00	open†	28	WDC-S	Ford Pass. '65	3.25	9.00	open†	28
WDC-DS	Ford Pass. '74	3.00	9.00	open†	28	WDC-T	Ford Pass. '65	3.50	9.00	open†	28
WDC-DT	Ford Pass. '74 Mercury '75	3.00	9.00	open†	28		Mercury '72	2.75	9.00	open†	28
WDC-DU	Ford Pass. '76 Mercury '75–76	3.00	9.00	open†	28	WDC-U	Ford Pass. '65 Mercury '65	3.89	9.00	open*†	28
WDC-DV	Mercury '75	3.25	9.00	open†	28		Mercury '72	2.75	9.00	open†	28
WDC-DW	Ford Pass. '75–77	3.00	9.00	open	28	WDC-V	Ford Pass. '65	4.11	9.00	open†	28
	Ford Pass. '78	2.75	9.00	open	28	WDC-W	Ford Pass. '65 Mercury '65	3.50	9.00	open†§	31
	Mercury '75–77	3.00	9.00	open	28	WDC-X	Ford Pass. '65 Mercury '65	4.11	9.00	open†§	31
	Mercury '78	2.75	9.00	open	28	WDC-Z	Mercury '65	3.00	9.00	open	28
WDC-DX	Ford Pass. '75–76 Mercury '75	3.00	9.00	open	28	WDD-B	Ford Pass. '65	3.00	8.75	open	28
WDC-DY	Ford Pass. '76 Mercury '76	2.75	9.00	open†	28	WDD-C	Ford Pass. '65	3.00	8.75	open*	28
WDC-DZ	Mercury '75–76	2.75	9.00	open†	28	WDD-D	Ford Pass. '65 Mercury '65	3.00	8.75	open	28
WDC-E	Ford Pass. '65	3.25	8.75	open*	28	WDD-E	Ford Pass. '65	3.50	8.75	open	28
WDC-EA	Ford Pass. '75–77 Mercury '75–77	2.75	9.00	open	28	WDD-F	Ford Pass. '65	3.50	8.75	open*	28
WDC-EB	Ford Pass. '76–78 Mercury '76–78	2.75	9.00	open	28	WDD-G	Ford Pass. '65	3.00	9.00	open*	28
						WDD-H	Ford Pass. '65	3.00	9.00	open	28
WDC-EE	Ford Pass. '76–78 Mercury '76–78	3.00	9.00	open	28	WDD-J	Ford Pass. '66	3.00	9.00	open*	28
WDC-EG	Ford Pass. '76–78 Mercury '76–78	3.00	9.00	open	28	WDD-K	Ford Pass. '66	3.50	8.75	open	28
						WDD-L	Ford Pass. '66	3.00	8.75	open	28
WDC-EH	Ford Pass. '76–78 Mercury '76–78	2.75	9.00	open	28	WDD-LX	Ford Pass. '66	3.00	8.75	open	28
						WDD-T	Ford Pass. '66	3.00	8.75	open	28

* pinion damper style flange   ** 1/2-inch ring gear bolts   † 4-pinion   § high performance

Code	Application/Year	Ratio (:1)	Ring Gear Diam (inches)	Diff Type	Axle Shaft Splines	Code	Application/Year	Ratio (:1)	Ring Gear Diam (inches)	Diff Type	Axle Shaft Splines
WDD-TX	Ford Pass. '66	3.00	8.75	open	28	WDM-AG2	F100 '73–79	3.00	9.00	open	31
WDD-U	Ford Pass. '66	3.25	8.75	open	28	WDM-AG3	F100 '73–79	3.00	9.00	open	28
WDE-A	T-Bird '64	3.00	9.00	l-slip			F150 '75–79				
WDE-B	T-Bird '65	3.00	9.00	l-slip	28	WDM-AG4	F100 '73–79	3.00	9.00	open	28
WDF-A	Van '63–67	4.11	9.00	l-slip	28		F150 '75–79				
WDF-B	Van '63–67	4.57	9.00	l-slip	28	WDM-AH	F100 '73–79	3.25	9.00	open	31
WDF-C	Van '63–67	3.50	9.00	l-slip	28		F150 '75–79				
WDF-D	Van '63–67	3.00	9.00	l-slip	28	WDM-AH2	F100 '73–79	3.25	9.00	open	31
WDF-E	Van '63–67	4.11	9.00	l-slip	28		F150 '75–79				
WDF-F	Van '63–67	4.57	9.00	l-slip	28	WDM-AJ	F100 '73–78	3.50	9.00	open	31
WDF-G	Van '63–67	3.50	9.00	l-slip	28	WDM-AJ1	F100 '73–78	3.50	9.00	open	31
WDF-H	Van '63–67	3.00	9.00	l-slip	28	WDM-AK	F100 '73–78	3.50	9.00	open	31
WDF-J	Van '63–67	4.11	9.00	l-slip	28	WDM-AK2	F100 '73–78	3.50	9.00	open	31
WDF-K	Van '63–67	4.57	9.00	l-slip	28	WDM-AL	F100 '73–75	3.70	9.00	open	28
WDF-L	Van '63–67	3.50	9.00	l-slip	28	WDM-AM	F100 '75–79	3.00	9.00	open	31
WDF-M	Van '63–67	3.00	9.00	l-slip	28	WDM-AM2	F100 '75–79	3.00	9.00	open	31
WDL-AA	Ford Pass. '68–69	2.75	9.00	l-slip	28	WDM-AN	F100 '73–79	3.25	9.00	open	31
	Mercury '68–69						F150 '75–79				
WDL-AB	Ford Pass. '68	3.00	8.75	l-slip	28	WDM-AN2	F100 '73–79	3.25	9.00	open	31
WDL-AC	Ford Pass. '68–69	3.25	8.75	l-slip	28		F150 '75–79				
WDL-AD	Ford Pass. '68	2.75	9.00	l-slip	28	WDM-AR	F100 '73–75	3.70	9.00	open	28
	Mercury '68					WDM-AS	F100 '73–78	3.50	9.00	open	28
WDL-AE	Ford Pass. '68–69	3.25	9.00	l-slip	28	WDM-AU	F150 '75–79	3.25	9.00	open	31
	Mercury '68–69					WDM-AU2	F150 '75–79	3.25	9.00	open	31
WDL-AF	Ford Pass. '69	2.75	9.00	l-slip†	28	WDM-AV	F100 '75–79	3.00	9.00	open	31
	Mercury '69						F150 '75–79				
WDL-AG	Ford Pass. '69	3.25	9.00	l-slip†	28	WDM-AV2	F100 '75–79	3.00	9.00	open	31
	Mercury '69						F150 '75–79				
WDL-B	Ford Pass. '65	3.25	8.75	l-slip	28	WDM-AY	F100 '73–79	3.25	9.00	open	31
WDL-C	Ford Pass. '65	3.25	8.75	l-slip*	28		F150 '75–79				
WDL-D	Ford Pass. '65	3.25	8.75	l-slip*	28	WDM-AY2	F100 '73–79	3.25	9.00	open	31
WDL-E	Ford Pass. '65	3.00	9.00	l-slip	28		F150 '75–79				
	Mercury '65					WDM-AY5	F100 '73–79	3.25	9.00	open	31
WDL-F	Ford Pass. '65	3.25	8.75	l-slip*	28		F150 '75–79				
WDL-G	Mercury '65	3.00	9.00	l-slip	28	WDM-AZ	F100 '73–78	3.50	9.00	open	31
WDL-H	Ford Pass. '65	3.50	8.75	l-slip	28	WDM-AZ2	F100 '73–78	3.50	9.00	open	31
WDL-K	Ford Pass. '65	3.25	9.00	l-slip	28	WDM-B	F150 '63–72	3.50	9.00	open	28
WDL-L	Ford Pass. '65	3.25	9.00	l-slip*	28	WDM-BA	F100 '73–78	3.50	9.00	open	31
WDL-M	Ford Pass. '66	3.25	8.75	l-slip	28	WDM-BA2	F100 '73–78	3.50	9.00	open	31
WDL-N	Ford Pass. '66–68	3.00	9.00	l-slip	28	WDM-BB	F100 '73–76	4.11	9.00	open	31
	Mercury '66–68					WDM-BC	Bronco '78	3.00	9.00	open†	31
WDL-P	Ford Pass. '66	3.50	8.75	l-slip	28		F100 '75–79				
WDL-W	Ford Pass. '66–69	3.00	8.75	l-slip	28		F150 '75–79				
WDL-WIX	Ford Pass. '67	3.00	8.75	l-slip	28	WDM-BC1	Bronco '78	3.00	9.00	open†	31
WDL-Z	Ford Pass. '67–68	3.25	8.75	l-slip	28		F100 '75–79				
WDL-ZX	Ford Pass. '67	3.25	8.75	l-slip	28		F150 '75–79				
WDM-A	F100 '63–71	3.25	9.00	open	28	WDM-BC2	Bronco '78	3.00	9.00	open†	31
WDM-AB	F100 '63–76	4.11	9.00	open	28		F100 '75–79				
WDM-AB1	F100 '73–76	4.11	9.00	open	31		F150 '75–79				
	F150 '75–79					WDM-BC5	Bronco '78	3.00	9.00	open†	31
WDM-AC	F100 '63–79	3.25	9.00	open	28		F100 '75–79				
WDM-AD	F100 '63–72	3.50	9.00	open	28		F150 '75–79				
WDM-AE	Bronco '78	3.50	9.00	open†	31	WDM-BD	F150 '75–79	3.50	9.00	open	31
	F100 '63–72	3.70	9.00	open†	28	WDM-BE	F150 '75–76	3.70	9.00	open	31
	F100 '73–78	3.50	9.00	open†	31	WDM-BF	F100 '75–79	3.00	9.00	open	28
	F150 '75–79					WDM-BF2	F100 '75–79	3.00	9.00	open	28
WDM-AF	F100 '63–79	3.25	9.00	open	28	WDM-BG	F100 '75–79	3.00	9.00	open	28
WDM-AG	F100 '63–78	3.00	9.00	open	28	WDM-BG2	F100 '75–79	3.00	9.00	open	28
WDM-AG1	F100 '73–79	3.00	9.00	open	31	WDM-BJ	F100 '77–79	2.75	9.00	open	31
	F150 '75–79		9.00	open	31		F150 '78–79				

* pinion damper style flange   ** 1/2-inch ring gear bolts   † 4-pinion   § high performance

Code	Application/Year	Ratio (:1)	Ring Gear Diam (inches)	Diff Type	Axle Shaft Splines
WDM-BJ2	F100 '77–79 / F150 '78–79	2.75	9.00	open	31
WDM-BJ5	F100 '77–79 / F150 '78–79	2.75	9.00	open	31
WDM-BK2	Bronco '80–86 / F150 '80–86	3.50	9.00	open	31
WDM-BM4	F100 '71–79	2.75	9.00	open	28
WDM-BR	F150 '78–79	2.75	9.00	open	31
WDM-BR5	F150 '78–79	2.75	9.00	open	31
WDM-BT	F100 '77–79 / F150 '78–79	2.75	9.00	open	31
WDM-BU2	F100 '77–79 / F150 '75–79	3.00	9.00	open	31
WDM-BU4	F100 '75–79 / F150 '75–79	3.00	9.00	open	31
WDM-BU5	F100 '75–79 / F150 '78–79	3.00	9.00	open	31
WDM-BV2	F100 '77–79 / F150 '78–79	2.75	9.00	open	31
WDM-BV4	F100 '77–79 / F150 '78–79	2.75	9.00	open	28
WDM-BV5	F100 '77–78 / F150 '78	2.75	9.00	open	31
WDM-BY2	F100 '73–79 / F150 '75–79	3.25	9.00	open	31
WDM-BZ	F100 '73–78 / F150 '75–79	3.50	9.00	open	31
WDM-C	F100 '63–72	3.70	9.00	open	28
	F100 '78	2.75	9.00	open	28
WDM-CA	Bronco '78 / F100 '75–79 / F150 '75–79	3.00	9.00	open†	31
WDM-CA	Bronco '78 / F100 '75–79 / F100 '75–79	3.00	9.00	open†	31
WDM-CB	F100 '77–79 / F150 '78–79	2.75	9.00	open	31
WDM-CC	F100 '77–78 / F150 '78	2.75	9.00	open	31
WDM-CC4	F100 '77–79	2.75	9.00	open	28
WDM-CD	F150 '75–79	3.50	9.00	open	31
WDM-CF	F100 '79–82 / F150 '79–82	3.00	9.00	Type	31
WDM-CG	F100 '79 / F150 '79	2.75	9.00	open	31
WDM-CH	Bronco '79	3.00	9.00	open†	31
WDM-CJ	F100 '79 / F150 '79	2.75	9.00	open	28
	F100 '80–82 / F150 '80–82		9.00	open	31
WDM-CK	F100 '79–82 / F150 '79–82	3.25	9.00	open	31
WDM-CL	F100 '79 / F150 '79	2.75	9.00	open	28
	F100 '80–82 / F150 '80–82		9.00	open	31
WDM-CM	F100 '79 / F150 '79	2.75	9.00	open	31
WDM-CN	Bronco '80–82 / F150 '79–82	3.50	9.00	open	31

Code	Application/Year	Ratio (:1)	Ring Gear Diam (inches)	Diff Type	Axle Shaft Splines
WDM-CR	Bronco '79	3.50	9.00	open†	31
WDM-D	F100 '63–72	4.11	9.00	open	28
WDM-DA	Bronco '80–82 / F100 '80–82 / F150 '80–82	3.00	9.00	open	31
WDM-DB	F100 '81–82	2.47	9.00	open	31
WDM-DB1	F100 '82	2.50	9.00	open	31
WDM-DC	F100 '81–82 / F150 '81–82	2.47	9.00	open	31
WDM-DD	F100 '81–82 / F150 '81–82	3.25	9.00	open	31
WDM-DL	Bronco '80–86 / F150 '80–86	3.25	9.00	open	31
WDM-DM	Bronco '80–86 / F150 '80–86	4.11	9.00	open	31
WDM-DR	Bronco '80–86 / F150 '80–86	3.00	9.00	open	31
WDM-E	F100 '63–72	3.25	9.00	open	28
WDM-F	F100 '63–72	3.50	9.00	open	28
WDM-H	F100 '63–72	3.25	9.00	open	28
WDM-J	F100 '63–72	3.50	9.00	open	28
WDM-K	F100 '63–72	3.70	9.00	open	28
WDM-L	F100 '63–72	4.11	9.00	open	28
WDM-M	F100 '63–72	3.50	9.00	open	28
WDM-R	F100 '63–72	4.11	9.00	open	28
WDM-S	F100 '63–72	3.25	9.00	open	28
WDM-T	F100 '63–78	3.50	9.00	open	28
WDM-T2	F100 '73–78	3.50	9.00	open	28
WDM-U	F100 '63–76	3.70	9.00	open	28
WDM-V	F100 '63–72	4.11	9.00	open	28
WDM-W	F100 '63–72	3.50	9.00	open	28
WDM-Z	F100 '63–72	4.11	9.00	open	28
WDN-A	F100 '63–72	3.70	9.00	open	28
WDN-B	F100 '63–72	3.50	9.00	open	28
WDN-C	F100 '63–72	3.70	9.00	open	28
WDN-D	F100 '63–72	3.50	9.00	open	28
WDN-J	F100 '63–72	4.11	9.00	open	28
WDO-M2	Mustang '71	3.25	9.00	l-slip†	28
WDR-A	F100 '63–72	4.11	9.00	open	28
WDR-B	F100 '63–72	4.11	9.00	open	28
	F100 '83 / F150 '83	2.73	8.50	open	31
WDS-BS	Ford Pass. '66	3.00	9.00	open	
WDW-K2	Comet '68 / Fairlane '68	2.75	9.00	open	28
WDX-A	Granada '75–76 / Monarch '75–76	2.75	9.00	open	28
WDX-B	Granada '75–76	3.00	9.00	open	28
WDX-D	Versailles '77–78	2.50	9.00	open	28
WDX-E	Versailles '77–78	2.75	9.00	open	28
WDX-F	Versailles '77	3.00	9.00	open	28
WDX-G	Versailles '78, to 3/15/78	2.50	9.00	open	28
	Versailles '78–80, from 3/15/78	2.47			
WDX-K	Versailles '79	2.75	9.00	open	28
WDX-L	Granada '80 / Monarch '80	2.47	9.00	open	28
WDX-M	Versailles '80	3.00	9.00	open	28
WDX-N	Versailles '80	2.75	9.00	open	28

* pinion damper style flange   ** 1/2-inch ring gear bolts   † 4-pinion   § high performance

Code	Application/Year	Ratio (:1)	Ring Gear Diam (inches)	Diff Type	Axle Shaft Splines	Code	Application/Year	Ratio (:1)	Ring Gear Diam (inches)	Diff Type	Axle Shaft Splines
WDX-R	Granada '80 Monarch '80	2.75	9.00	open	28	WEB-BH	Cougar '77 Cougar '78, early	2.50	9.00	open	28
WEB-A	Montego '74	3.00	9.00	open†	28		Cougar '78, late Cougar '79	2.47	9.00	open	28
	Torino '74	3.25	9.00	open†	28		LTD II '77 LTD II '78, early	2.50	9.00	open	28
WEB-AA	Comet '69 Fairlane '69–70 Montego '70–71 Torino '71	3.25	9.00	open†	31		LTD II '78, late LTD II '79	2.47	9.00	open	28
WEB-AD	Cougar '74 Montego '72–74 Torino '72–74	2.75	9.00	open	28	WEB-BJ	Cougar '76–78 LTD II '77–78 Montego '76 Torino '76	3.00	9.00	open	28
WEB-AE	Montego '72	3.00	9.00	open	28	WEB-BK	Cougar '78 LTD II '78	3.00	9.00	open	28
WEB-AF	Montego '72–76 Torino '72–76	3.25	9.00	open†	28	WEB-BL	Cougar '76–78 LTD II '77–78 Montego '76 Torino '76	3.00	9.00	open	28
WEB-AG	Montego '72–76 Torino '72–76	3.00	9.00	open	28	WEB-BM	Cougar '77–78 LTD II '77–78	2.75	9.00	open	28
WEB-AH	Cougar '74–76 Montego '72–76 Torino '72–76	3.25	9.00	open†	28	WEB-BN	LTD II '77–79	2.75	9.00	open	28
WEB-AJ	Montego '72–73	3.00	9.00	open	28	WEB-BR	Cougar '78–79 LTD II '78–79	3.00	9.00	open	28
	Torino '73–74	3.00	9.00	l-slip	28	WEB-BS	Cougar '78 LTD II '78	2.50	9.00	open	28
WEB-AM	Torino '72	3.25	9.00	open	28	WEB-BT	Cougar '78 LTD II '78	2.75	9.00	open	28
WEB-AM5	Montego '73–74 Torino '73–74	2.75	9.00	open	28	WEB-C	Comet '66–67 Fairlane '66–67	3.25	9.00	open	28
WEB-AN	Montego '73 Torino '73	3.00	9.00	open†	28	WEB-E	Comet '67–69 Fairlane '66–70 Montego '70	3.00	9.00	open†	28
WEB-AR	Couger '75–76 Montego '73–76 Torino '73–76	3.25	9.00	open†	28	WEB-F	Comet '67–69 Fairlane '66–69	3.25	9.00	open†	28
WEB-AS	Montego '74–76	3.00	9.00	open†	28	WEB-G	Comet '67 Fairlane '67	3.89	9.00	open†§	31
WEB-AT	Cougar '74–76 Montego '74–76	2.75	9.00	open†	28	WEB-H	Comet '67–69 Fairlane '67–70 Montego '70–71 Torino '71	2.75	9.00	open	28
WEB-AU	Montego '74–76 Torino '74–76	2.75	9.00	open†	28	WEB-J	Comet '67–68 Fairlane '67–68	2.75	9.00	open†	28
WEB-AV	Cougar '74–76 Montego '74–76 Torino '74–76	3.00	9.00	open	28	WEB-K	Comet '68 Fairlane '68	3.25	9.00	open†§	31
WEB-AY	Cougar '74–76 Montego '74–76 Torino '74–76	3.00	9.00	open†	28	WEB-L	Comet '68–69 Fairlane '69–70 Montego '70–71 Torino '72	3.50	9.00	open†	31
WEB-AZ	Torino '74	2.75	9.00	open†	28	WEB-M	Comet '69 Fairlane '69–70 Montego '70–71 Torino '72	3.00	9.00	open†	28
WEB-B	Comet '66–67 Fairlane '66–67		9.00	open	28	WEB-N	Comet '69	3.00	9.00	open	
WEB-BA	Montego '74 Torino '74	2.75	9.00	open	28	WEB-P	Comet '69 Fairlane '69	2.75	9.00	open†	28
WEB-BB	Montego '74 Torino '74	2.75	9.00	open†	28	WEB-R	Comet '69 Fairlane '69–70 Montego '70–71 Torino '72	3.00	9.00	open	28
WEB-BC	Cougar '75–79 LTD II '77–78 Montego '75–76 Torino '75–76	2.75	9.00	open	28	WEB-S	Comet '69 Fairlane '69	3.25	9.00	open	28
WEB-BD	LTD II '77–78 Montego '75–76 Torino '75–76	2.75	9.00	open	28						
WEB-BF	Cougar '77 Cougar '78, early	2.50	9.00	open	28						
	Cougar '78, late Cougar '79	2.47	9.00	open	28						
	LTD II '77 LTD II '78, early	2.50	9.00	open	28						
	LTD II '78, late LTD II '79	2.47	9.00	open	28						

* pinion damper style flange   ** 1/2-inch ring gear bolts   † 4-pinion   § high performance

Code	Application/Year	Ratio (:1)	Ring Gear Diam (inches)	Diff Type	Axle Shaft Splines	Code	Application/Year	Ratio (:1)	Ring Gear Diam (inches)	Diff Type	Axle Shaft Splines
WEB-T	Comet '69 Fairlane '69–70 Montego '70–71 Torino '72	3.25	9.00	l-slip†	28	WED-A	Comet '66–68 Fairlane '66–67	3.25			
WEB-U	Comet '69	3.25	9.00	open		WED-A1	Fairlane '66–67	3.25	9.00	l-slip	28
WEB-Z	Comet '69 Fairlane '69–70 Montego '70	3.00	9.00	open†	31	WED-A4	Fairlane '66–68	3.25	9.00	l-slip†	28
						WED-A5	Fairlane '66–68	3.25	9.00	l-slip†	28
WEC-A	Comet '66–67 Fairlane '66–67	3.00	9.00	open	28	WED-A6	Fairlane '66–68	3.25	9.00	l-slip†	28
WEC-AA	Torino '74	3.25	9.00	open†	28	WED-C	Comet '66–67 Fairlane '66–67	3.00	9.00	l-slip	28
WEC-AB	Torino '72	3.00	9.00	open	28	WED-D	Comet '66–68 Fairlane '66–68	3.00	9.00	l-slip†	28
WEC-AC	Montego '73–74 Torino '73–74	3.50	9.00	open†	28	WED-D7	Comet '69	3.25	9.00	l-slip†	
WEC-AD	Montego '73–76 Torino '73–76	3.00	9.00	open†	28	WED-E	Comet '68 Fairlane '68	3.50	9.00	l-slip†	28
WEC-AF	Montego '74 Torino '74	3.50	9.00	open†	28	WED-F	Fairlane '66–69 Falcon '66–69	3.25	9.00	l-slip	28
WEC-AG	Montego '72 Torino '72	3.00	9.00	open	28	WEE-A	Comet '66–67 Fairlane '66	3.25	9.00	l-slip	28
WEC-AH	Montego '72 Torino '72	3.25	9.00	open†	28	WEE-C	Comet '66–67 Fairlane '66–67	3.00	9.00	l-slip	28
WEC-B	Comet '66–67 Fairlane '66–67	3.25	9.00	open	28	WEE-D	Comet '66–68 Fairlane '66–68	3.00	9.00	l-slip†	28
	Van '83–85 E250	3.55	8.50	open	31	WEE-D5	Comet '68	3.00	9.00	l-slip†	
WEC-BZ	T-Bird '67	3.00	9.00	open		WEE-D6	Comet '69	3.25	9.00	l-slip†	
WEC-D	Comet '67–69 Fairlane '66–70	3.00	9.00	open†	28	WEM-A	Bronco '66–70	4.11	9.00	open	28
						WEM-A2	Bronco '70–73	4.11	9.00	open	28
WEC-E	Comet '67–69 Fairlane '66–69	3.25	9.00	open†	28	WEM-A3	Bronco '74–76	4.11	9.00	open	28
WEC-F	Comet '67 Fairlane '67	2.75				WEM-B	Bronco '66–69	4.11	8.75	l-slip	28
						WEM-BIX	Bronco '67	4.11	8.75	l-slip	28
WEC-G	Fairlane '67	2.75	9.00	open†	28	WEM-C	Bronco '66–73	4.57	9.00	open	28
WEC-H	Comet '69 Fairlane '69–70	3.00	9.00	open†	28	WEM-C2	Bronco '66–73	4.57	9.00	open	28
						WEM-C3	Bronco '74	4.57	9.00	open	28
WEC-J	Comet '69	3.00	9.00	open		WEM-D	Bronco '66–67	4.57	9.00	l-slip	28
WEC-K	Comet '69 Fairlane '69–70 Montego '70–71 Torino '72	3.00	9.00	open	28	WEM-E	Bronco '66–73	3.50	9.00	open	28
						WEM-E2	Bronco '66–73	3.50	9.00	open	28
						WEM-E3	Bronco '74–77	3.50	9.00	open	28
WEC-L	Comet '69 Fairlane '69–70 Montego '70–71 Torino '72	3.25	9.00	open†	28	WEM-F	Bronco '66–69	3.50	8.75	l-slip	28
						WEM-FIX	Bronco '67	3.50	8.75	l-slip	28
						WEN-A	Bronco '66–70	4.11	9.00	open	28
WEC-N	Comet '69 Fairlane '69	3.25	9.00	open	28	WEN-A2	Bronco '66–70	4.11	9.00	open	28
							Bronco '70–72	4.11	9.00	open	28
WEC-R	Comet '69 Fairlane '69–70 Montego '70–71	3.50	9.00	open†	31	WEN-B	Bronco '66–69	4.11	8.75	l-slip	28
						WEN-BIX	Bronco '67	4.11	8.75	l-slip	28
						WEN-C	Bronco '66–67	4.57	9.00	open	28
WEC-S	Comet '69 Fairlane '69–70 Montego '70–71 Torino '72	3.25	9.00	open†	31	WEN-D	Bronco '66–67	4.57	9.00	open	28
						WEN-E	Bronco '66–70	3.50	9.00	open	28
						WEN-E2	Bronco '66–70	3.50	9.00	open	28
							Bronco '70–72	3.50	9.00	open	28
WEC-T	Montego '71 Torino '71	3.00	9.00	open†	31	WEN-F	Bronco '66–69	3.50	8.75	l-slip	28
						WEN-FIX	Bronco '67	3.50	8.75	l-slip	28
WEC-V	Cougar '73–74 Montego '72–74 Torino '72–74	3.50	9.00	open†	28	WES-AA	Cougar '69–71 Mustang '69–71	3.00	9.00	open	28
						WES-AB	Cougar '69–71 Mustang '69–71	3.25	9.00	open	28
						WES-AC	Cougar '69–71 Mustang '69–70	3.00	9.00	open†	28
WEC-Z	Montego '72–74 Torino '72–73	3.25	9.00	open†	28	WES-AD	Cougar '69–73 Mustang '69–73	3.25	9.00	open†	28
						WES-AE	Cougar '69–71 Mustang '69–72	3.50	9.00	open†	31
						WES-AG	Cougar '69–70 Mustang '69–71	2.75	9.00	open†	28

* pinion damper style flange	** 1/2-inch ring gear bolts	† 4-pinion	§ high performance

Code	Application/Year	Ratio (:1)	Ring Gear Diam (inches)	Diff Type	Axle Shaft Splines	Code	Application/Year	Ratio (:1)	Ring Gear Diam (inches)	Diff Type	Axle Shaft Splines
WES-AH	Cougar '69–70 Mustang '69–71	3.00	9.00	open†	31	WEV-AL	Van '79–81 E100 Van '79–81 E150	3.25	9.00	open	28
WES-AJ	Cougar '69–71 Mustang '69–71	3.25	9.00	open†	31	WEV-AL1	Van '81–83 E100 Van '81–83 E150	3.25	9.00	open	31
WES-AJ2	Cougar '69–71 Mustang '69–71	3.25	9.00	open†	31	WEV-AR	Van '80–81 E100 Van '80–81 E150	2.75	9.00	open	28
WES-AJ3	Cougar '71 Mustang '71	3.25	9.00	open†	28	WEV-AR1	Van '81–83 E100 Van '81–83 E150	2.75	9.00	open	31
WES-AK	Couger '72–73 Mustang '71–73	3.50	9.00	open†	28	WEV-AT	Van '80–81 E100 Van '80–81 E150	2.75	9.00	open	28
WES-D	Cougar '67	3.00	9.00	open		WEV-AU	Van '81 E100 Van '81 E150	2.47	9.00	open	28
WES-E	Cougar '67	3.00	9.00	l-slip		WEV-AU1	Van '81–83 E100 Van '81–83 E150	2.47	9.00	open	31
WES-F	Cougar '67–69 Mustang '67–70	3.00	9.00	open†	28	WEV-AV	Van '83 E100 Van '83 E150	3.50	9.00	open	31
WES-G	Cougar '67–68 Mustang '67–69	3.25	9.00	l-slip†	28	WEV-AZ	Van '83 E100 Van '83 E150	3.50	9.00	open	31
WES-H	Cougar '67–68	3.50	9.00	open†§	28	WEV-B	Van '68–72 E100	3.00	9.00	open	28
WES-J	Cougar '67	3.89	9.00	open†§	28	WEV-C	Van '68–72 E100	4.11	9.00	open	28
WES-K	Cougar '67	3.50	9.00	open†§	28	WEV-G	Van '68–72 E100 Van '78–79 E100 Van '78–79 E150	3.25	9.00	open	28
WES-M	Cougar '68–70 Mustang '68–70	3.25	9.00	open†§	28	WEV-G1	Van '68–72 E100 Van '78–79 E100 Van '78–79 E150	3.25	9.00	open	28
WES-N	Cougar '69 Mustang '68	3.00	8.75	open	28						
WES-P	Cougar '69 Mustang '68	3.25	8.75	open	28	WEV-G3	Van '73–75 E100 Van '75 E150	4.11	9.00	open	28
WES-R	Mustang '68	3.25	8.75	l-slip	28	WEV-H	Van '73–75 E100	3.70	9.00	open	28
WES-S	Cougar '68 Mustang '68–69	2.75	9.00	open†	28	WEV-L	Van '73–77 E100 Van '75–77 E150	3.00	9.00	open	28
WES-T	Cougar '69–73 Mustang '69–73	2.75	9.00	open	28	WEV-M	Van '75 E150	4.11	9.00	open	28
WES-U	Cougar '68 Mustang '68–69	3.50	9.00	open†	31	WEV-N	Van '73–77 E100 Van '75–78 E150	3.50	9.00	open	28
WES-V	Mustang '68	3.00	8.75	l-slip	28	WEV-R	Van '73–78 E100 Van '75–78 E150	3.00	9.00	open	28
WES-Y	Cougar '68 Mustang '68	3.50	9.00	l-slip†	31	WEV-S	Van '75–76 E100	3.00	9.00	open	28
WES-Z	Cougar '68 Mustang '68	3.00	9.00	l-slip†	28	WEV-T	Van '73–78 E100	3.50	9.00	open	28
WEV-A	Van '68–77 E100 Van '75–79 E150	3.50	9.00	open	28	WEW-A	Van '68–74 E200	4.11	9.00	open	28
WEV-AA	Van '73–78 E100 Van '75–78 E150	2.75	9.00	open	28	WEW-B	Van '68–72 E200	4.57	9.00	open	28
WEV-AB	Van '78–79 E100 Van '78–79 E150	2.75	9.00	open	28	WEW-C	Van '68–74 E200	3.50	9.00	open	28
						WEW-D	Van '68–72 E200	3.00	9.00	open	28
WEV-AC	Van '78–79 E100 Van '78–79 E150	3.25	9.00	open†	28	WEW-J	Van '68–74 E200	3.25	9.00	open	28
WEV-AD	Van '73–77 E100 Van '75–78 E150	3.50	9.00	open	28	WEW-K	Van '68–74 E200	3.70	9.00	open	28
WEV-AE	Van '78–79 E100 Van '78–79 E150	2.75	9.00	open	28	WFA-A	Comet '69 Fairlane '69	3.25	9.00	l-slip†	28
WEV-AG	Van '78–79 E100 Van '78–79 E150	2.75	9.00	open	28	WFA-AA	Couger '74–78 LTD II '77–78 Montego '74–76 Torino '74–76	3.00	9.00	l-slip†	28
WEV-AH	Van '79 E100	2.75	9.00	open	28	WFA-AB	Montego '74 Torino '74	2.75	9.00	l-slip†	28
WEV-AJ	Van '79–81 E150 Van '80–81 E100	3.00	9.00	open	28	WFA-AD	Cougar '76 Montego '76 Torino '76	2.75	9.00	l-slip†	28
WEV-AJ1	Van '81–83 E100 Van '81–83 E150	3.00	9.00	open	31	WFA-AE	Cougar '76 Montego '76 Torino '76	2.75	9.00	l-slip†	28
WEV-AK	Van '79–81 E100 Van '79–81 E150	2.75	9.00	open	28	WFA-AF	Cougar '77 LTD II '77	2.50	9.00	l-slip†	28
WEV-AK1	Van '81–83 E100 Van '81–83 E150	2.75	9.00	open	31						

* pinion damper style flange ** 1/2-inch ring gear bolts † 4-pinion § high performance

Code	Application/Year	Ratio (:1)	Ring Gear Diam (inches)	Diff Type	Axle Shaft Splines	Code	Application/Year	Ratio (:1)	Ring Gear Diam (inches)	Diff Type	Axle Shaft Splines
WFA-AG	Cougar '77 / LTD II '77	2.50	9.00	l-slip†	28	WFB-A	Cougar '69–70 / Mustang '69–70	3.25	9.00	l-slip†	28
WFA-AH	LTD II '77 / Montego '76 / Torino '76	3.00	9.00	l-slip†	28	WFB-AM	Versailles '77	2.75	9.00	l-slip†	28
WFA-AK	Cougar '77 / LTD II '77	2.50	9.00	l-slip†	28	WFB-C	Cougar '69–73 / Mustang '69–73	3.25	9.00	l-slip†	28
WFA-AL	Cougar; early '77–79, to 10/15/78	2.75	9.00	l-slip†	28	WFB-D	Cougar '69–72 / Mustang '69–72	3.00	9.00	l-slip†	28
	Cougar; late '79, from 10/15/78		9.00	l-slip	28	WFB-D2	Cougar '72–73 / Mustang '72–73	2.75	9.00	l-slip†	28
	LTD II; '77–early '79, to 10/15/78		9.00	l-slip†	28	WFB-E	Granada '75–78 / Monarch '75–76	3.00	9.00	l-slip	28
	LTD II; late '79, from 10/15/78		9.00	l-slip	28	WFB-F	Granada '75–78 / Monarch '75–76	3.00	9.00	l-slip	28
WFA-B	Comet '69 / Fairlane '69	3.00	9.00	l-slip†	28	WFB-G	Granada; early '77–78, to 3/15/78	2.50	9.00	l-slip	28
WFA-C	Comet '69 / Fairlane '69	3.25	9.00	l-slip†	28		Granada; late '78, from 3/15/78	2.47	9.00	l-slip	28
WFA-D	Comet '69 / Fairlane '69–70 / Montego '70–71 / Torino '71	3.25	9.00	l-slip†	28		Monarch; early '77–78, to 3/15/78	2.50	9.00	l-slip	28
WFA-E	Comet '69 / Fairlane '69–70 / Montego '70–71 / Torino '71	3.25	9.00	l-slip†	28		Monarch; late '78, 3/15/78	2.47	9.00	l-slip	28
WFA-G	Comet '69 / Fairlane '69–70	3.00	9.00	l-slip†	28	WFB-G1	Granada '77–78	2.50	9.00	l-slip	28
WFA-H	Comet '69 / Montego '70–71 / Torino '71	3.00	9.00	l-slip†	28	WFB-K	Granada '77–78 / Versailles '77–78	2.50	9.00	l-slip†	28
WFA-J	Fairlane '70 / Montego '70	3.00	9.00	l-slip†	28	WFB-L	Versailles '77	2.50	9.00	open	28
WFA-L	Montego '72 / Torino '72	3.00 / 3.25	9.00 / 9.00	l-slip† / open†	28 / 28	WFB-M	Versailles '77	2.75	9.00	open	28
WFA-L4	Cougar '73–74 / Montego '72–74 / Torino '72–76	2.75	9.00	l-slip†	28	WFC-A	Capri '81–82	3.08	7.50	l-slip	28
							Comet '69	3.50	9.00	l-slip†	31
WFA-L5	Cougar '73–74 / Montego '72–74 / Torino '72–76	2.75	9.00	l-slip†	28		Cougar '81–82	3.08	7.50	l-slip	28
							Fairlane '69	3.50	9.00	l-slip†	31
WFA-M	Montego '72–76 / Torino '72–76	3.25	9.00	l-slip†	28		Fairmont '81–82 / Granada '81–82	3.08	7.50	l-slip	28
WFA-N	Montego '72–73 / Torino '72–73	3.00	9.00	l-slip†	28		Lincoln Continental '82	3.08	7.50	l-slip	28
WFA-R	Cougar '75–76 / Montego '72–76 / Torino '72–76	3.25	9.00	l-slip†	28		Mustang '81–82 / T-Bird '81–82 / Zephyr '81–82	3.08	7.50	l-slip	28
WFA-S	Montego '72–73 / Torino '72–73	3.00	9.00	l-slip†	28	WFC-AA	Cougar '83 / Montego '74 / T-Bird / Torino '74	3.08 / 3.50 / 3.08	9.00	l-slip†	28
WFA-V	Montego '73–76 / Torino '73–76	2.75	9.00	l-slip†	28	WFC-B	Capri '81–83	3.08	7.50	l-slip	28
							Comet '68–69	3.91	9.00	l-slip†	
WFA-Y	Cougar '75 / Montego '73–75 / Torino '73–76	3.25	9.00	l-slip†	28		Fairlane '68–70	3.91	9.00	l-slip†	
							Fairmont '81–82	3.08	7.50	l-slip	28
							Lincoln Continental '82	3.08	7.50	l-slip	28
WFA-Z	Cougar '74078 / LTD II '77–78 / Montego '74–76 / Torino '74–76	3.00	9.00	l-slip†	28		Montego '70	3.91	9.00	l-slip†	
							Mustang '81–83	3.08	7.50	l-slip	28
							Zephyr '81–83	3.08	7.50	l-slip	28
						WFC-C	Capri '81–82	3.45	7.50	l-slip	28
							Comet '68–69	4.30	9.00	l-slip†	31
							Fairlane '68–70	4.30	9.00	l-slip†	31
							Fairmont '81–82	3.45	7.50	l-slip	28
							Montego '70	4.30	9.00	l-slip†	31
							Mustang '81–82	3.45	7.50	l-slip	28
							Zephyr '81–82	3.45	7.50	l-slip	28
						WFC-C5	Lincoln & Town Car '74	2.75	9.00	l-slip†	28

* pinion damper style flange   ** 1/2-inch ring gear bolts   † 4-pinion   § high performance

Code	Application/Year	Ratio (:1)	Ring Gear Diam (inches)	Diff Type	Axle Shaft Splines	Code	Application/Year	Ratio (:1)	Ring Gear Diam (inches)	Diff Type	Axle Shaft Splines
WFC-D	Capri '81–88	2.73	7.50	l-slip	28	WFC-L3	Montego '71	3.50	9.00	l-slip†	28
	Comet '69	3.91	9.00	l-slip†	31		Torino '71				
	Fairlane '69	3.91	9.00	l-slip†	31	WFC-L5	Cougar '73–74	3.50	9.00	l-slip†	28
	Fairmont '81–86	2.73	7.50	l-slip	28		Montego '73–74				
	Lincoln	2.73	7.50	l-slip	28		Torino '73–74				
	Continental '82					WFC-M	Fairlane '69	3.00	9.00	l-slip†	31
	Mustang '81–86	2.73	7.50	l-slip	28		Ranger '83	3.45	7.50	l-slip	28
	Zephyr '81–86	2.73	7.50	l-slip	28	WFC-N	Fairlane '70	3.25	9.00	l-slip†	31
WFC-E	Capri '82–86	2.73	7.50	l-slip	28		Montego '70–71				
	Cougar '82–86	2.73	7.50	l-slip	28		Torino '71				
	Fairlane '69	3.91	9.00	l-slip†	31	WFC-N3	Montego '71	3.25	9.00	l-slip†	28
	Fairmont '82–86	2.73	7.50	l-slip	28		Torino '71				
	Granada '82–86	2.73	7.50	l-slip	28	WFC-R	Capri '82–84	3.08	7.50	l-slip	28
	Lincoln	2.73	7.50	l-slip	28		Fairlane '70	3.25	9.00	l-slip†	31
	Continental '82						Montego '70–71	3.25	9.00	l-slip†	31
	Mustang '82–86	2.73	7.50	l-slip	28		Mustang '82–84	3.08	7.50	l-slip	28
	T-Bird '82	2.73	7.50	l-slip	28		Torino '71 3.25	3.25	9.00	l-slip†	31
	Zephyr '82–86	2.73	7.50	l-slip	28	WFC-R3	Montego '71	3.25	9.00	l-slip†	28
WFC-F	Capri '82	3.45	7.50	l-slip	28		Torino '71				
	Comet '69	3.91	9.00	l-slip†	31	WFC-S	Cougar '82	3.08	7.50	l-slip	28
	Cougar '82	3.45	7.50	l-slip	28		Montego '71	3.25	9.00	l-slip†	28
	Fairlane '69–70	3.91	9.00	l-slip†	31		Torino '71	3.25	9.00	l-slip†	28
	Fairmont '82	3.45	7.50	l-slip	28	WFC-S3	Montego '71	3.00	9.00	l-slip†	28
	Granada '82	3.45	7.50	l-slip	28		Torino '71				
	Lincoln	3.45	7.50	l-slip	28	WFC-T	Montego '72–74	3.25	9.00	l-slip†	28
	Continental '82						Torino '72–74				
	Montego '70	3.91	9.00	l-slip†	31	WFC-U	Torino '74	3.25	9.00	l-slip†	28
	Mustang '82	3.45	7.50	l-slip	28	WFC-Y	Montego '73–76	3.00	9.00	l-slip†	28
	Zephyr '82	3.45	7.50	l-slip	28		Torino '73–76				
WFC-G	Capri '82	3.08	7.50	l-slip	28	WFC-Z	Montego '73	3.50	9.00	l-slip†	28
	Comet '69	3.00	9.00	l-slip†	31		Torino '73				
	Cougar '82	3.08	7.50	l-slip	28	WFC-Z5	Torino '74	3.25	9.00	open†	28
	Fairlane '69–70	3.00	9.00	l-slip†	31	WFD-A	Cougar '69–72	3.91	9.00	l-slip†	31
	Fairmont '82	3.08	7.50	l-slip	28		Mustang '69–73				
	Granada '82	3.08	7.50	l-slip	28	WFD-B	Cougar '68–70	3.91	9.00	l-slip†	31
	Lincoln	3.08	7.50	l-slip	28		Mustang '68–70				
	Continental '82					WFD-C	Cougar '68–70	4.30	9.00	l-slip†	31
	Montego '70	3.00	9.00	l-slip†	31		Mustang '68–70				
	Mustang '82	3.08	7.50	l-slip	28	WFD-D	Cougar '69–72	3.91	9.00	l-slip†	31
	T-Bird '82	3.08	7.50	l-slip	28		Mustang '69–73				
	Zephyr '82	3.08	7.50	l-slip	28	WFD-E	Cougar '69–70	4.30	9.00	l-slip†	31
WFC-J	Capri '82–83	3.08	7.50	l-slip	28		Mustang '69–70				
	Comet '69	3.50	9.00	l-slip†	31	WFD-F	Cougar '69–71	3.50	9.00	l-slip†	31
	Cougar '82	3.08	7.50	l-slip	28		Mustang '69–71				
	Fairlane '69–70	3.50	9.00	l-slip†	31	WFD-FZ	Cougar '69–71	3.50	9.00	l-slip†	31
	Fairmont '82–83	3.08	7.50	l-slip	28		Mustang '69–71				
	Granada '82–83	3.08	7.50	l-slip	28	WFD-F3	Cougar '71–73	3.50	9.00	l-slip†	28
	Lincoln	3.08	7.50	l-slip	28		Mustang '71–73				
	Continental '82					WFD-J	Cougar '69	3.25	9.00	l-slip†	31
	Montego '70–73	3.50	9.00	l-slip†	31		Mustang '69				
	Mustang '82–83	3.08	7.50	l-slip	28	WFD-K	Cougar '69–70	3.00	9.00	l-slip†	31
	T-Bird '82	3.08	7.50	l-slip	28		Mustang '69–70				
	Torino '71–74	3.50	9.00	l-slip†	31	WFD-L	Cougar '69–70	3.00	9.00	l-slip†	31
WFC-K	Comet '69	4.30	9.00	l-slip†	31		Mustang '69–70				
	Fairlane '69					WFD-M	Cougar '70–71	3.25	9.00	l-slip†	31
WFC-L	Comet '69	3.50	9.00	l-slip†	31		Mustang '70–71				
	Fairlane '69–70	3.50	9.00	l-slip†	31	WFD-M2	Cougar '70–71	3.25	9.00	l-slip†	31
	Montego '70–72	3.50	9.00	l-slip†	31		Mustang '70–71				
	Torino '71	3.50	9.00	l-slip†	31	WFD-M3	Cougar '71	3.25	9.00	l-slip†	28
	Torino '72	3.50	9.00	l-slip†	28		Mustang '71				

* pinion damper style flange　　　　** 1/2-inch ring gear bolts　　　　† 4-pinion　　　　§ high performance

Code	Application/Year	Ratio (:1)	Ring Gear Diam (inches)	Diff Type	Axle Shaft Splines	Code	Application/Year	Ratio (:1)	Ring Gear Diam (inches)	Diff Type	Axle Shaft Splines
WFD-R	Granada '76 Monarch '76	3.00	8.00	l-slip	28	WFE-N	F150 '75–79	3.50	9.00	l-slip	31
WFE-A	F100 '69–76	3.70	9.00	l-slip	28	WFE-R	F150 '76	3.70	9.00	l-slip	31
WFE-AB	F150 '75–79	3.25	9.00	l-slip	31	WFE-S	F100 '73–79 F150 '75–79	3.25	9.00	l-slip	31
WFE-AC	F100 '73–79 F150 '75–79	3.25	9.00	l-slip	31	WFE-T	F100 '73–79 F150 '75–79	3.25	9.00	l-slip	31
WFE-AD	F100 '75–79 F150 '75–79	3.00	9.00	l-slip	28	WFE-V	Bronco '78	4.11	9.00	l-slip†	31
WFE-AF	F100 '73–79 F150 '77–79	3.00	9.00	l-slip	28	WFE-V1	Bronco '78	4.11	9.00	l-slip†	31
WFE-AG	F100 '77–79 F150 '78–79	2.75	9.00	l-slip	28	WFE-V2	F150 '75–79	4.11	9.00	l-slip	31
WFE-AH	F100 '77–79 F150 '78–79	2.75	9.00	l-slip	28	WFE-V3	F150 '75–79	4.11	9.00	l-slip	31
WFE-AK	F150 '75–79	3.50	9.00	l-slip	31	WFE-V3	F150 '75–79	4.11	9.00	l-slip	31
WFE-AR	F150 '78–79	4.11	9.00	l-slip	31	WFE-V5	F150 '75–79	4.11	9.00	l-slip	31
WFE-AS	F150 '76–79	3.50	9.00	l-slip	31	WFG-A	Ford Pass. '70–74 Mercury '70–74	2.75	9.00	l-slip	28
WFE-AU	F100 '78–79 F150 '78–79	3.25	9.00	l-slip	31	WFG-AA	Ford Pass. '74–78 Mercury '74–78	2.75	9.00	l-slip†	28
WFE-AV	F100 '79–82	2.75	9.00	l-slip	31	WFG-AB	Ford Pass. '74–76 Mercury '74–76	3.25	9.00	l-slip†	28
WFE-AW	Bronco '80–82 F150 '79–82	3.50	9.00	l-slip	31	WFG-AC	Mercury '74	2.75	9.00	l-slip†	28
WFE-AX	F150 '79	4.11	9.00	l-slip	31	WFG-AD	Mercury '74–76	3.25	9.00	l-slip†	28
WFE-AY	Bronco '79	3.50	9.00	l-slip†	31	WFG-AE	Ford Pass. '74–76 Mercury '74–76	3.00	9.00	l-slip	28
WFE-AZ	Bronco '79	4.11	9.00	l-slip†	31	WFG-AF	Ford Pass. '74 Mercury '74	2.75	9.00	l-slip	28
WFE-B	Bronco '78 F100 '69–72	4.11 / 3.25	9.00	l-slip† / l-slip	31 / 28	WFG-AG	Ford Pass. '74–76 Mercury '74–76	3.00	9.00	l-slip†	28
WFE-BA	F100 '80–82 F150 '80–82	2.75	9.00	l-slip	31	WFG-AH	Ford Pass. '74	3.00	9.00	l-slip†	28
WFE-BBA	F100 '82	2.75	9.00	l-slip	31	WFG-AK	Ford Pass. '74	3.00	9.00	l-slip†	28
WFE-BC	F100 '81–82 F150 '81–82	3.00	9.00	l-slip	31	WFG-AL	Ford Pass. '76–78 Mercury '75–78	3.00	9.00	l-slip†	28
WFE-BD	F100 '81–82 F150 '81–82	3.25	9.00	l-slip	31	WFG-AM	Mercury '75	3.25	9.00	l-slip†	28
WFE-BE	F100 '82	2.75	9.00	l-slip	31	WFG-AN	Ford Pass. '76 Mercury '75–76	2.75	9.00	l-slip†	28
WFE-BL	Bronco '80–86 F150 '80–86	4.11	9.00	l-slip	31	WFG-AR	Mercury '75–76	2.75	9.00	l-slip	28
WFE-BN	Bronco '80–86 F150 '80–86	3.00	9.00	l-slip	31	WFG-AS	Ford Pass. '75–76 Mercury '75–76	2.75	9.00	l-slip	28
WFE-C	F100 '69–72	3.50	9.00	l-slip	28	WFG-AT	Ford Pass. '75–76 Mercury '75–76	2.79	9.00	l-slip	28
WFE-D	F100 '69–72	4.11	9.00	l-slip	28	WFG-AU	Ford Pass. '75–76 Mercury '75–76	3.00	9.00	l-slip	28
WFE-E	Bronco '78 F100 '73–78 F150 '75–79	3.50	9.00	l-slip†	31	WFG-AZ	Ford Pass. '76–78 Mercury '76	2.75	9.00	l-slip	28
WFE-E1	Bronco '78 F100 '73–78 F150 '75–79	3.50	9.00	l-slip†	31	WFG-B	Granada '77 Monarch '77	2.50	9.00	l-slip†	28
WFE-E2	F100 '73–78 F150 '75–79	3.50	9.00	l-slip	31	WFG-BA	Ford Pass. '76 Mercury '76	3.25	9.00	l-slip	28
WFE-E5	F100 '73–78 F150 '75–78	3.50	9.00	open	31	WFG-BD	Ford Pass. '76	2.75	9.00	l-slip	28
WFE-F	F100 '73–78 F150 '75–79	3.50	9.00	l-slip	31	WFG-BG	Mercury '76	2.75	9.00	l-slip†	28
WFE-G	F100 '73–76	4.11	9.00	l-slip	31	WFG-BH	Ford Pass. '77 Mercury '77	3.00	9.00	l-slip†	28
WFE-H	F100 '73–76	4.11	9.00	l-slip	31	WFG-BJ	Ford Pass. '77 Mercury '77–78	2.75	9.00	l-slip†	28
WFE-J	F100 '73–76 F150 '75	3.50	9.00	l-slip	31	WFG-BK	Ford Pass. '77 Mercury '78	2.47	9.00	l-slip†	28
WFE-K	F100 '75–79	3.00	9.00	l-slip	31	WFG-BK1	Ford Pass. '78 Mercury '78	2.50	9.00	l-slip†	28
WFE-L	F100 '73–79	3.25	9.00	l-slip	31	WFG-BL	Ford Pass. '78 Mercury '78	2.50	9.00	l-slip†	28
WFE-M	F100 '73–76	3.70	9.00	l-slip	28	WFG-BM	Ford Pass. '78 Mercury '78	2.75	9.00	l-slip	28

* pinion damper style flange   ** 1/2-inch ring gear bolts   † 4-pinion   § high performance

Code	Application/Year	Ratio (:1)	Ring Gear Diam (inches)	Diff Type	Axle Shaft Splines
WFG-C	Ford Pass. '70–74 / Mercury '70–74	3.25	9.00	l-slip	28
WFG-D	Ford Pass. '70–72 / Mercury '70–72	2.75	9.00	l-slip	28
WFG-E	Ford Pass. '70–73 / Mercury '70–74	3.25	9.00	l-slip†	28
WFG-G	Ford Pass. '70–72 / Mercury '70–72	3.00	9.00	l-slip†	28
WFG-H	Mercury '72	2.75	9.00	l-slip†	28
WFG-J	Ford Pass. '72 / Mercury '72	3.00	9.00	l-slip	28
WFG-K	Mercury '72	3.00	9.00	l-slip	28
WFG-K5	Ford Pass. '74	2.75	9.00	l-slip†	28
	Mercury '73–76	3.00	9.00	l-slip	28
WFG-L	Mercury '72	3.00	9.00	l-slip†	28
WFG-M	Ford Pass. '73 / Mercury '73	2.75	9.00	l-slip	28
WFG-N	Mercury '73–74	3.25	9.00	l-slip†	28
WFG-R	Ford Pass. '73–78 / Mercury '73–77	3.00	9.00	l-slip†	28
WFG-S	Mercury '73–74	2.75	9.00	l-slip†	28
WFG-T	Mercury '73	2.75	9.00	l-slip†	28
WFG-U	Mercury '74	3.25	9.00	l-slip†	28
WFG-Y	Ford Pass. '73–76 / Mercury '73–76	3.00	9.00	l-slip	28
WFG-Z	Ford Pass. '74–76 / Mercury '74–76	3.25	9.00	l-slip	28
WFK-D	Montego '73–74 / Torino '73–74	3.25	9.00	l-slip	28
WFP-A	Bronco '70–73	4.11	9.00	l-slip	28
WFP-B	Bronco '70–73	3.50	9.00	l-slip	28
WFR-A	Bronco '70–76	4.11	9.00	l-slip	28
WFR-A3	Bronco '77	4.11	9.00	l-slip	28
WFR-B	Bronco '70–76	3.50	9.00	l-slip	28
WFR-B	Bronco '70–76	3.50	9.00	l-slip	28
WFR-B3	Bronco '77	3.50	9.00	l-slip	28
WFR-C	Bronco '73–76	4.11	9.00	l-slip	28
WFR-D	Bronco '73–76	3.50	9.00	l-slip	28
WFS-A	Van '83 E250	3.55	8.50	l-slip	31
WFS-B	Van '83 E250	3.55	8.50	l-slip	31
	Maverick '70–71	3.00	8.00	l-slip	28
WFS-C	Comet '71 / Maverick '71	3.00	8.00	l-slip	28
WFT-AZ	Van '83 E100 / Van '83 E150	3.50	9.00	l-slip	31
WFT-D	Van '75–78 E100	3.50	9.00	l-slip	28
	Van '75 E100 / Van '75 E150	4.11	9.00	l-slip	28
WFT-F	Van '78–79 E100 / Van '78–79 E150	3.25	9.00	l-slip	28
WFT-G	Van '78–79 E100 / Van '78–79 E150	2.75	9.00	l-slip	28
WFT-H	Van '75–79 E100 / Van '75–79 E150	3.00	9.00	l-slip	28
WFT-L	Van '79–81 E100 / Van '79–81 E150	2.75	9.00	l-slip	28
WFT-L1	Van '81–83 E100 / Van '81–83 E150	2.75	9.00	l-slip	31
WFT-M	Van '79 E100 / Van '79 E150	3.25	9.00	l-slip	28
WFT-T	Van '80–81 E100 / Van '80–81 E150	3.25	9.00	l-slip	28
WFT-U	Van '81 E100 / Van '81 E150	3.00	9.00	l-slip	28
WFT-U1	Van '81–83 E100 / Van '81–83 E150	3.00	9.00	l-slip	31
WFT-V	Van '83 E100 / Van '83 E150	3.50	9.00	l-slip	31
WFU-D	Fairlane '70 / Montego '70	4.30	9.00	l-slip	31
WFU-E	Cougar '70 / Mustang '70	4.30	9.00	l-slip	31
WFU-E1	Cougar '71 / Mustang '71	4.11	9.00	l-slip†	31
WFU-F	Cougar '70	4.30	9.00	l-slip	31
WFV-A	T-Bird '70–75	2.75	9.00	l-slip†	28
WFV-A4	T-Bird '70–75	2.75	9.00	l-slip†	28
WFV-A5	Lincoln Mark Series '74	3.25	9.00	l-slip†	28
	T-Bird '73–75	2.75	9.00	l-slip†	28
WFV-B	T-Bird '70–71	3.00	9.00	l-slip†	28
	Lincoln Mark Series '74	3.25	9.00	l-slip†	28
	T-Bird '73–74				
WFV-C	T-Bird '72	3.00	9.00	l-slip†	28
WFV-D	Lincoln Mark Series '73–76 / T-Bird '72–76	2.75	9.00	l-slip†	28
WFV-E	Lincoln Mark Series '73 / T-Bird '72–73	3.00	9.00	l-slip†	28
WFV-F	Lincoln Mark Series '73–74 / T-Bird '72–74	3.25	9.00	l-slip†	28
WFV-H	T-Bird '74	2.75	9.00	l-slip†	28
WFV-L	T-Bird '74–76	3.00	9.00	l-slip†	28
WFV-M	Lincoln Mark Series '74–76 / T-Bird '74–76	3.00	9.00	l-slip†	28
WFV-N	T-Bird '75–76	2.75	9.00	l-slip†	28
WFV-P	Lincoln Mark Series '75–76 / Lincoln Mark Series '77–78 / T-Bird '75–76	3.00	9.00	l-slip†	28
WFV-R	T-Bird '76	2.75	9.00	l-slip†	28
WFV-S	Lincoln Mark Series '77	3.00	9.00	l-slip†	28
WFV-T	Lincoln Mark Series; early '77–79, to 10/15/78	2.75	9.00	l-slip†	28
	Lincoln Mark Series; late '79, from 10/15/78	2.75	9.00	l-slip†	28
WFV-U	Lincoln Mark Series; early '78, to 5/1/78	2.50	9.00	l-slip†	28
	Lincoln Mark Series; late '78, from 5/1/78	2.47	9.00	l-slip†	28
WFY-A	Ford Pass. '77 / Lincoln & Town Car '72 / Lincoln & Town Car '74–79	2.75	9.00	l-slip†	28
WFY-A5	Ford Pass. '77 / Lincoln & Town Car '72 / Lincoln & Town Car '74–79	2.75	9.00	l-slip†	28

* pinion damper style flange   ** 1/2-inch ring gear bolts   † 4-pinion   § high performance

Code	Application/Year	Ratio (:1)	Ring Gear Diam (inches)	Diff Type	Axle Shaft Splines
WFY-A1	Lincoln & Town Car; early '73–79, to 10/15/78	2.75	9.00	l-slip†	28
	Lincoln & Town Car; late '79, from 10/15/78		9.00	l-slip	28
WFY-B	Lincoln & Town Car '72	2.75	9.00	l-slip†	28
WFY-B1	Lincoln & Town Car '73–75	3.00	9.00	l-slip†	28
WFY-B5	Lincoln & Town Car '73–75	3.00	9.00	l-slip†	28
WFY-C	Lincoln & Town Car '73	2.75	9.00	l-slip†	28
WFY-D	Lincoln & Town Car '72	2.75	9.00	l-slip†	28
WFY-E	Lincoln & Town Car '72	3.00	9.00	l-slip†	28
WFY-F	Lincoln & Town Car '74–76	3.00	9.00	l-slip†	28
WFY-G	Lincoln & Town Car '75–76	3.00	9.00	l-slip†	28
WFY-H	Lincoln & Town Car '76	2.75	9.00	l-slip†	28
WFY-K	Lincoln & Town Car '77–78	3.00	9.00	l-slip†	28
WFY-N	Lincoln & Town Car '77	3.00	9.00	l-slip†	28
WGB-AA	Lincoln Mark Series '76–77 T-Bird '76	3.00	9.00	open	28
WGB-AB	Lincoln Mark Series; early '77-'78, to 5/1/78, Mark V	2.50	9.00	open	28
	Lincoln Mark Series; late '78–79 from 5/1/78, Mark V	2.47	9.00	open	28
WGB-AC	Lincoln Mark Series '76–78 T-Bird '76	3.00	9.00	open	28
WGB-AD	Lincoln Mark Series '77–79	2.75	9.00	open	28
WGB-C	T-Bird '70–72	2.75	9.00	open†	28
WGB-D	T-Bird '70–71	3.00	9.00	open†	28
WGB-D3	T-Bird '72–74	3.25	9.00	open†	28
WGB-D4	T-Bird '72–74	3.25	9.00	open†	28
WGB-D5	T-Bird '72–74	3.25	9.00	open†	28
WGB-E	T-Bird '72–73	2.75	9.00	open	28
WGB-F	T-Bird '72	3.00	9.00	open	28
WGB-G	T-Bird '72–75	2.75	9.00	open†	28
WGB-H	T-Bird '72	3.00	9.00	open†	28
WGB-J	T-Bird '72–73	2.75	9.00	open	28
WGB-K	Lincoln & Town Car '77	2.50	9.00	open	28
WGB-K5	Lincoln Mark Series '73–76 T-Bird '72–76	2.75	9.00	open†	28
WGB-L	T-Bird '72–73	3.00	9.00	open	28
WGB-M	Lincoln Mark Series '73	3.00	9.00	open†	28
WGB-N	Lincoln Mark Series '72–74	3.25	9.00	open†	28
WGB-T	T-Bird '74–75	3.00	9.00	open†	28
WGB-U	Lincoln Mark Series '74–78 T-Bird '74–76	3.00	9.00	open†	28
WGB-V	Lincoln Mark Series '75–79	2.75	9.00	open†	28
WGB-K	Lincoln Mark Series '77	2.50	9.00	open	28
WGB-K5	Lincoln Mark Series '73–76 T-Bird '72–76	2.75	9.00	open†	28
WGB-L	T-Bird '72–73	3.00	9.00	open	28
WGB-M	Lincoln Mark Series '73	3.00	9.00	open†	28
WGB-N	Lincoln Mark Series '72–74	3.25	9.00	open†	28
WGB-T	T-Bird '74–75	3.00	9.00	open†	28
WGB-U	Lincoln Mark Series '74–78 T-Bird '74–76	3.00	9.00	open†	28
WGB-V	Lincoln Mark Series '75–79 T-Bird '75–76	2.75	9.00	open†	28
WGB-W	Lincoln Mark Series '75–77	3.00	9.00	open†	28
	Lincoln Mark Series '78–79	3.00	9.00	open	28
	T-Bird '75–76	3.00	9.00	open†	28
WGB-X	Lincoln Mark Series '77 T-Bird '76	2.75	9.00	open†	28
WGB-Y	T-Bird '76	3.00	9.00	open†	28
WGC-A	Lincoln Mark Series '78–79 Lincoln & Town Car '72–75	2.75	9.00	open†	28
WGC-B	Lincoln & Town Car '72–75	2.75	9.00	open	28
		3.00	9.00	open	28
WGC-B1	Lincoln & Town Car '73–78	3.00	9.00	open†	28
WGC-B5	Lincoln & Town Car '73–78	3.00	9.00	open†	28
WGC-C	Lincoln & Town Car '73–78	2.75	9.00	open†	28
WGC-D	Lincoln & Town Car '73–78	3.00	9.00	open†	28
WGC-G	Lincoln & Town Car '75–78	2.75	9.00	open†	28
WGC-H	Lincoln & Town Car '75–78	3.00	9.00	open†	28
WGC-J	Lincoln & Town Car '76–78	3.00	9.00	open	28
WGC-K	Lincoln & Town car; early '77–78, to 3/15/78	2.50	9.00	open	28
	Lincoln & Town Car, late '78–79, from 3/15/78	2.47	9.00	open	28
WGC-L	Lincoln & Town Car '76–78	2.75	9.00	open	28
WGC-M	Lincoln & Town Car '76–78	3.00	9.00	open	28
WGC-N	Lincoln & Town Car '77–78	2.75	9.00	open†	28
WGC-R	Lincoln & Town Car '79	3.00			

* pinion damper style flange　　　　** 1/2-inch ring gear bolts　　　　† 4-pinion　　　　§ high performance

SOURCE GUIDE

9-inch Factory
100 Axle Dr.
Caspian, MI 49915
800-332-3450
www.9inchfactory.com

Currie Enterprises
382 N. Smith
Corona, CA 92880
714-528-6957
www.currieenterprises.com

Hellwig Products Co., Inc.
16237 Ave. 296
Visalia, CA 93292
800-435-5944
www.hellwigproducts.com

Mark Williams Enterprises
765 S. Pierce Ave.
Louisville, CO 80027
866-508-6394
www.markwilliams.com

McLeod Racing, LLC
1600 Sierra Madre Cir.
Placentia, CA 92870
714-630-2764
www.mcleodracing.com

Moser Engineering
102 Perfromance Dr.
Portland, IN 47371
260-726-6689
www.moserengineering.com

Ratech Manufacturing, Inc.
1110 Adwood Dr.
Cincinnati, OH 45240
513-742-2111
www.ratechmfg.com

Richmond Gear
1001 W. Exchange Ave.
Chicago, IL 60609
864-843-9275
www.richmondgear.com

Strange Engineering
8300 N. Austin Ave.
Morton Grove, IL 60053
847-663-1701
www.strangeengineering.net

Tremec
14700 Helm Ct.
Plymouth, MI 48170
800-401-9866
www.tremec.com

TrueHi9
www.truehi9.com

Williams Classic Chassis Works
2974 First St., Unit H
La Verne, CA 91750
909-392-1358
www.williamsclassicchassis.net